"This book is both timely and needed. Provocative, yes, because the message is essential at this decisive 'hinge moment' in time."

—Philip Yancey,
Author, *Vanishing Grace*

"This book arrives a crucially important time in history, as the chasm grows ever wider between who Christians say we are versus how the world perceives us. *The Way Back* is a much-needed wake up call for the Church to return to the humble and joy-filled basics of our faith. We've wandered for far too long."

—Christine Caine,
Author, Evangelist, and co-founder, A21

"I can't think of a single Christian in any walk of life who would not benefit from the insights and guidance found in *The Way Back*, but especially pastors, teachers, and communicators need this book, as does any executive trying to connect with Christians in America."

—Hugh Hewitt,
Nationally Syndicated Radio Host and MSNBC Host

"Phil Cooke and Jonathan Bock have shown in their book, *The Way Back* that traditional, core Christian values are not dated; in fact, they are more relevant today than ever before. I believe that this insightful, powerful, and provocative book will transform the way we believe and how we practice our beliefs!"

—DeVon Franklin,
Producer and *New York Times* Bestselling author

"In *The Way Back*, authors Phil Cooke and Jonathan Bock have tackled one of the most consequential issues of our time: how the Church can regain credibility, and, ultimately, authority to influence and move the needle of culture as it once did. We are all called to live like Jesus, and this book is the 'how-to' guide on how to do so in today's media-driven culture."

—Rev. Samuel Rodriguez,
President, National Hispanic Christian Leadership Conference,
Executive Producer of *The Impossibles*

"In *The Way Back*, my good friends Jonathan Bock and Phil Cooke have challenged how I think about the modern-day church and our need for a paradigm shift. In the same way, you'll be challenged to discard conventional thinking in favor of a bolder way of living, just like the first Christians. You'll also be inspired to hold fast to the Biblical values of the Early Church while pushing for innovation so we can regain influence and transform the world!"

—Bobby Gruenewald,
Pastor, Innovation Leader, Life.Church,
and Founder, YouVersion Bible App

"With facts and figures these authors force us to consider how American Christianity has become a reflection of our dominant culture, rather than being an instrument of God for changing it. Then, they go on to give us a vision of how we might recover that transforming influence we once had. I give this book two thumbs up."

—Tony Campolo,
Ph.D., Eastern University

"Phil and Jonathan's book *The Way Back* is so important right now. It's a wake-up call to remind us that the way we live our lives has an impact on others. If you want to make a difference in the world today, then this is the book to read."

—Roma Downey,
Actor, Producer, and President, LightWorkers Media

"*The Way Back* is a great recall book. Recall the way it was when the church was effective and reclaim the way the faithful can be effective in a challenging environment for the church. Proud of the gospel and aware of how the church has lost sight of itself in the recent past, this book is a wonderful response to how to find our way back to vibrancy."

—Darrell L. Bock,
Executive Director for Cultural Engagement,
Howard G. Hendricks Center and Senior Research Professor
of New Testament Studies, Dallas Theological Seminary

"I am thankful for the powerful message in *The Way Back*. If you're a Christian leader seeking to understand society and how to best reach people to further the Kingdom, you need this book. It truly dives in to how we, as leaders, can change the perception of today's culture toward Christians and Christianity and live lives of love that will force people to rethink what they think about Jesus. "

—Tyler Reagin,
President, Catalyst

"In this timely and essential book, well-liked and highly respected marketing experts, Phil Cooke and Jonathan Bock turn their decades of know-how towards solving the mounting public relations crisis that is holding back and sidelining many Christians today. Let *The Way Back* provide a roadmap for your way forward in impacting culture."

—Brad Lomenick,
Founder, BLINC, Former President of Catalyst,
and Author, *H3 Leadership* and *The Catalyst Leader*

"An insightful and devastating analysis of why Christians are ignored and irrelevant in our culture. But thankfully, Bock and Cooke's book offers lots of practical answers and examples of how to give ourselves away and find our way back. Very encouraging and hopeful."

—Ralph Winter,
Film Producer of *X-Men, Wolverine, Planet of the Apes*, and *Star Trek*

"I'm focusing a significant part of my future to raising up a new generation of Christian leaders who will share the gospel boldly, while understanding the changing culture we live in today. *The Way Back* could be a textbook for that cause. From two respected media and marketing experts, this is a wake-up call for the Body of Christ, and my great hope is that the Church will listen to the alarm."

—Dr. Jack Graham,
Senior Pastor, Prestonwood Church,
and founder, PowerPoint Media Ministries

"Phil Cooke and Jonathan Bock provide a unique and fresh perspective on evangelism for today's church. I really believe this is the kind of message that is going to transform how we approach the gospel, church, and people. I would encourage everyone to read this book—and to buy a copy for a family member or friend!"

—Pastor Chad Veach,
Lead Pastor, ZOE Church Los Angeles

"In *The Way Back*, Phil and Jonathan remind us that we are part of a winning team and the Gospel of Jesus is the ultimate prize. This book will reinvigorate believers to start trusting again in our own product and embolden us take that message to the masses in new, creative ways."

—Craig Gross,
Founder, XXXchurch.com

In Phil and Jonathan's book, *The Way Back*, they take a no-holds-barred look into how we've lost our influence in the world and give life-changing advice and insight into how we can find our way back to living a life that sets us, and the world, on fire again. I encourage you read this book with the mindset that each one of us needs to take an honest evaluation of ourselves and be bold in taking the steps we need to find our way again."

—Rob Hoskins,
President & CEO, OneHope, Inc.

"I have known Jonathan Bock and Phil Cooke for nearly 20 years now. I love that these two marketing experts are turning their attention to the Church and asking hard questions of why the Church has lost its impact on culture. Instead of focusing on modern marketing techniques, they are taking us back two thousand years to reclaim the essence that made the Church an unstoppable force. *The Way Back* is the way forward."

—Erwin Raphael McManus,
Founder, Mosaic, and Author, *The Last Arrow*

"*The Way Back* is an inspiring call to faith rather than fear. Phil Cooke and Jonathan Bock draw upon the winsome witness of the ancient church to forge a future for contemporary Christians. *The Way Back* is loaded with beautiful examples of how we can serve our communities today."

—Craig Detweiler,
President, The Seattle School of Theology and Psychology

"Seldom do leaders respond to a gentle tap. Most leaders engrossed in exploration and new conquests need a jarring experience to slow down, absorb, rethink, and realign. My friends Phil Cooke and Jonathan Bock do just that. The possibilities are real, achievable and practical. I want to be a part of "The Way Back" movement and so will you."

—Sam Chand,
Leadership Consultant and Author, *Bigger Faster Leadership*

"With authenticity and secure commitment to Christ, my friends Phil Cooke and Jonathan Bock have intentionally taken the bull by the horns, confronting believers everywhere to set out toward *The Way Back*: to not only believing but boldly living the all-powerful gospel we preach to the world. Their passion to see the Church and believers everywhere reflect Christ and engage zealously with society will both challenge your convictions and embolden your faith."

—Brian Houston,
Global Senior Pastor of Hillsong Church

"When you contrast the early Christians' power to turn the world upside down to the anemic weakness of Christianity today, you have to ask what went wrong and how to fix it. *The Way Back* explores that question and provides answers. Both Phil and Jonathan are uniquely qualified to navigate these waters. Get this book. Read it."

—Jerry A. Johnson, Ph.D.
President and CEO, National Religious Broadcasters

The
WAY
BACK

How Christians Blew Our Credibility
and HOW WE GET IT BACK

Phil Cooke and Jonathan Bock

#TheWayBack

WORTHY®
PUBLISHING

Published by Worthy Books, an imprint of Worthy Publishing Group, a division of Worthy Media, Inc., One Franklin Park, 6100 Tower Circle, Suite 210, Franklin, TN 37067.

WORTHY is a registered trademark of Worthy Media, Inc.

Helping people experience the heart of God

eBook available wherever digital books are sold.

Cataloging-in-Publication Data is on file with the Library of Congress.

For foreign and subsidiary rights, contact rights@worthypublishing.com

Published in association with Books & Such Literary Management, 52 Mission Circle, Suite 122, PMB 170, Santa Rosa, CA 95409, www.booksandsuch.com

ISBN: 978-1-61795-861-8

Cover Design: Melissa Reagan
Cover Image: Getty Images, Stockbyte
Interior Design and Typesetting: Bart Dawson

Printed in the United States of America
18 19 20 21 22 LBM 9 8 7 6 5 4 3 2

CONTENTS

This book is dedicated to fellow travelers searching for the way home.

Keep climbing.

You're not alone.

When God wants to change the world,
he doesn't send in the tanks.
He sends in the meek.

N. T. WRIGHT,
SIMPLY JESUS

Perhaps the question should not be:
"Why are others persecuted?"
Perhaps the better question is:
"Why are we not?"

NIK RIPKEN,
THE INSANITY OF GOD

ACKNOWLEDGMENTS

IF YOU'VE EVER plopped yourself down in front of a computer to write a book, then you know it's no casual jog. More like an IRONMAN competition. In a barren desert.

This book is the culmination of no less than dozens of campfire conversations with thoughtful and frustrated Christian pals and more than a few wounded but helpful non-Christian friends. They helped us diagnose both the problems and the solutions. If we've learned nothing else from this experience, it's that many of the world's biggest problems can probably be solved around a fire pit.

We'd also be remiss not to thank our wives, Kathleen Cooke and Kelly Bock. You get the finished product, but they get the daily "Honey, what do you think if this?" globs of literary mush that eventually become a book. Simply put, without their patience and feedback, this endeavor would not have been possible.

Our literary agent, Rachelle Gardner, understood the concept immediately and was willing to do battle to help us find the right publisher. She did exactly that with Byron Williamson and Jeana Ledbetter at Worthy Publishing, who somehow saw the kernel of an idea and worked very hard to help us bring it to reality.

Finally, our editor, Jennifer Stair, did a masterful job helping us craft the final manuscript. She challenged us, inspired us, and helped two media and marketing guys craft a book that, hopefully, helps right the listing ship.

FOREWORD
BY ERIC METAXAS

I WILL NEVER, ever forget it. I was sitting at a wooden table in a restaurant in a small town in Germany called Wittenberg. My wife, Susanne, was with me and we were in fact across the street from the very spot upon which Martin Luther had posted his fabled 95 Theses five hundred years before!

In May 2017 I was there with Matt and Laurie Crouch to film a special program for their Trinity Broadcasting Network on the subject of Luther, and to celebrate the unavoidably important five-hundreth anniversary since the start of the Reformation. I had just finished writing a biography of Luther, *Martin Luther: The Man Who Rediscovered God and Changed the World,* and the Crouches thought having me there with them in Wittenberg would work well for their program on Luther—not to mention it would be a lot of fun!

And it certainly was fun, mainly because Matt Crouch has a streak of irreverent humor much like my own. We were able to crack jokes while talking about one of the most important figures in the history of the world. But another reason it was fun was because of what happened as we were sitting in the restaurant. This part you could not make up, even if you wanted to.

As the four of us sat there resting from a full day of filming—ordering our *kaffee und strudel, mit Schlagsahne, (natürlich, warum nicht?)*—I was either making a joke or a sarcastic comment when Matt said for the *second time* in as many days how much I reminded him of our mutual longtime friend, Phil Cooke. Phil is a media producer and consultant and he, too, has a streak of irreverent humor, and, somehow, my humor reminded Matt of Phil.

Phil lives in Los Angeles and I live in New York City, so I guess when two people are serious about their faith, have a streak of irreverent humor, work in media, and live in important coastal cultural capitals, others tend to think of you with respect to each other. (I might add here that Phil's lovely wife, Kathleen, recently told me that people sometimes call me the East Coast Phil Cooke, although we all know that in fact it is Phil Cooke who is the West Coast Eric Metaxas!)

In any event, we were all sitting at this table in Germany when it happened. I looked up from my strudel and saw something mightily perplexing. Was what I saw an apparition or a trick of the light? Or perhaps it was an optical illusion brought on by jetlag from my transatlantic flight? Indeed, it was none of these things. Into the obscure restaurant in Wittenberg, Germany walked in none other than Phil Cooke himself!

I almost fell out of my chair. Matt Crouch almost fell out of his chair too. We sat there, transfixed, staring agog at the supreme oddity of seeing the very person we were just discussing. The same someone who lives in very faraway Los Angeles. However inconceivable it was, it was all quite real and undeniable. After we realized we were not dreaming, we all stood up and ran over and said hello to Phil and Kathleen, and of course told Phil that we were, quite literally, just talking about him!

Naturally, we had to ask why Phil and Kathleen were in *Lutherstadt*, as Wittenberg is often called, and they told us that they were in this renowned city because Museum of the Bible was doing a special exhibition right down the street and Phil was filming the exhibit. None of us will ever forget that extraordinary moment.

But precisely what do this uncanny meeting—and Luther's Reformation—have to do with this book you are now reading?

For many years, Phil's work has been focused on engaging today's disrupted, media-driven world with the gospel. Part of his challenge is exploring the uncomfortable truths about why Christianity continues to lose influence in our culture. That's why he began working on this book with his friend and co-writer, Jonathan Bock. While I'm friends with Phil, I only know Jonathan by reputation—but as you may know, it's quite a reputation! He pioneered the concept of faith-based marketing in Hollywood, and every studio and network in town is his client. Maybe you've heard of one or two of the five hundred projects he's worked on: *The Lord of the Rings* trilogy, *The Chronicles of Narnia* films, *The Blind Side*, *Les Misérables*, *Bruce Almighty*, *The Conjuring* series, *The Bible* series on the History Channel, the *Finding Jesus* series on CNN, *Unbroken*, *The Book of Eli*, *42*, and *Walk the Line*. Working in Hollywood while maintaining the respect and admiration of the Christian community is no easy feat, but Jonathan somehow manages to pull it off.

If you are following my logic, Luther's Reformation—and what he did five hundred years earlier across the street from that restaurant where we ran into Phil—was precisely along the same lines as what this very book is about. You see, the Augustinian monk named Martin Luther was trying to get the church of his day to see that they had strayed from their original purpose. And he was hoping to get them to recalculate their position and head back to the place they had started from. Is this not the American church's dilemma today? Is that five-hundred-year-old story not our story this minute too? Let me blurt out the answer right now: *it is!*

Let's face it, church: we've strayed. And there's nothing to do but admit it and make our way back to where we ought to be. Why continue to waste time far from where we belong when we can begin the journey back to the spot where we ought to be? That was the crazy idea Luther had back then, and it is the crazy idea Phil, Jonathan, and many others have today. Their book is about the very idea that it is possible to get back to our roots and once again make a difference in this world.

So, won't you stop reading this foreword and start reading the book itself? In fact, I will give you no choice but to do just that—thank you for reading this far, but don't stop! Phil and Jonathan's message is very important. God bless you as you read.

ERIC METAXAS
NEW YORK CITY
OCTOBER 2017

THE DISCONNECT

The Christian faith is quickly losing traction
in Western culture, not only as a result of
unchristian behavior, as significant as that is,
but because we haven't recognized
our new reality and adapted.

GABE LYONS,
THE NEXT CHRISTIANS

We are a nation that is unenlightened
because of religion. I do believe that.
I think religion stops people from thinking.
I think it justified crazies.

COMEDIAN BILL MAHER

IN A 2013 *Wall Street Journal* interview, Russell Moore, president of the Southern Baptist Convention's Ethics & Religious Liberty Commission, shared the story of a college friend who wanted to run for political office two decades ago, so the choice of which church to attend was a critical first step. In those days, a potential senator or governor needed to join a local church because everyone else belonged. But today, his friend wouldn't feel that way at all, because the need to be associated with a Christian church has largely disappeared from society. In fact, today, church attendance is almost a hindrance to running for public office, since people of other faiths—or no faith at all—might be offended. Moore said, "The Bible Belt is collapsing."

Most Christians would probably agree. Often, it feels like the world we knew is headed in the wrong direction. A few years ago, a news aggregator website listed incidents of an America seemingly gone mad. You might have heard some of these stories in the news:

- A federal judge threatened "incarceration" to a high school valedictorian unless she removed references to Jesus from her graduation speech.
- City officials prohibited senior citizens from praying over their meals, listening to religious messages, or singing gospel songs at a senior activities center.

- A public university's law school banned a Christian organization because it required its officers to adhere to a statement of faith that the university disagreed with.
- The US Department of Justice argued before the Supreme Court that the federal government can tell churches and synagogues which pastors and rabbis it can hire and fire.
- The State of Texas sought to approve and regulate what religious seminaries can teach.
- The US Department of Veterans Affairs banned the mention of God from veterans' funerals, overriding the wishes of the deceaseds' families.

These days, such stories feel like common occurrences, don't they? A slow, drip-drip erosion of Christian faith in the public square—legal attacks on the Boy Scouts, stores discouraging employees from saying "Merry Christmas," or some public monument needing to be removed because it dared mention God in the marble—makes it feel as if our faith is slipping away.

Statistically, there has been an unmistakable drop in the number of people claiming to be Christians. An eye-opening report from the Pew Research Center indicates that the number of Americans identifying as "Christian" has slipped 8 percent in the last seven years. And as if that weren't enough, the number of those who claim to follow no religion at all (called "nones") is dramatically rising.

When statistics like this are combined with the general

sinking feeling of waning Christian influence on culture, it's easy to feel as if the air is coming out of the balloon.

**Faith leaders call it the decline
of American Christianity.
College professors call it post-Christian.
Secularists call it long overdue.**

As two media and marketing professionals who are committed Christians, it's frustratingly obvious to us that our faith has a pronounced disconnect with the potential audience of nonbelievers. And while there is no shortage of facts and figures to back up this truth, deep down in your gut you know it too.

The Bible famously lays out a laundry list of nine qualities we, as believers, are to be known for. They are called the "fruit of the Spirit" (Galatians 5:22–23):

- Love
- Joy
- Peace
- Patience
- Kindness
- Goodness
- Faithfulness
- Gentleness
- Self-Control

Yet when you look at words non-Christians regularly use to describe us, our fruits seem a bit rotten:

- Hypocritical
- Judgmental
- Harsh
- Power-Hungry
- Phony
- Insensitive
- Bigoted
- Reactionary
- Exclusive

The chasm between how Christians see ourselves and how non-Christians in our culture see us—that's the perception problem. But is this a death spiral for our faith, or is it a fixable issue? That's where the journey started for us.

Quick, get the marketing guys on the phone!

SEE IT THROUGH OUR EYES

Because we both have spent decades in the media business, we essentially look at everything through the lens of marketing. Jonathan is a marketing and public relations executive and the founder of Grace Hill Media, a firm that not only markets film and television but also advises Hollywood studios and entertainment companies about reaching the Christian audience. Major movies such as *The Chronicles of Narnia, The Blind Side, Unbroken, Walk the Line,* and *Bruce Almighty,* and television shows such as *The Bible* and *Finding Jesus,* were successful in part because Jonathan's team understands the Christian mind-set and what Christian audiences are looking for (or not looking for) when it comes to entertainment. Jonathan also produced *Hillsong—Let Hope Rise,* the story of the popular worship band Hillsong UNITED.

Phil is a writer, filmmaker, media consultant, and cofounder of Cooke Pictures, a media production company that advises and produces programming for some of the most influential churches, Christian ministries, and nonprofit organizations in the country. In an interview, former CNN reporter Paula Zahn joked that Phil was rather rare—a working producer in Hollywood with a PhD in theology. Phil's primary focus has been helping Christians engage today's distracted, media-driven culture more effectively, and his books, like *Unique: Telling Your Story in the Age of Brands and Social Media,* are road maps for anyone sharing a message of faith in the cluttered and distracted world we live in today. Phil and Jonathan worked together as executive producers of Hillsong—Let Hope Rise and on many other major projects.

Both of us work at the intersection of faith, media, and culture. Most of our clients and projects are focused on reaching the greatest number of people with what we believe is the ultimate message of hope. As a result, we spend a lot of time exploring (and sometimes arguing about) how to make that happen.

This book is the result of those discussions—particularly in light of the question: *What do we do about the decline of Christianity in today's culture?*

There are plenty of academic papers and books on apologetics, cultural criticism, and theology that tell us how we got into this mess. Those are important, but coming from the perspective of marketing and media, we're all about *action.* What can we *do* to find the way back?

The goal of this book is to answer: *How can we change the perception of today's culture toward Christians and Christianity?*

"Actually, I preferred 'Heaven' too, but then the marketing guys got a hold of it."

Like all overly confident media people, we think *every* problem can be solved by better marketing. Is your house small? Call it "cozy." Have too many job changes on that résumé? Well, your experiences are "wide-ranging." Can't get enough customers to your restaurant? That's because you're "exclusive." So it probably doesn't surprise you that we initially thought the perception problem of our faith would be solved *by changing our culture's perceptions.*

But we're not saying that facetiously.

We're not just hired guns selling trail mix one day and religion the next. We're both 100 percent committed followers of Jesus. We both believe that faith is the last best hope for a crumbling world, and that Christianity has been a net gain for culture during the last two thousand years.

The Bible is the single most important document ever written. Our faith has birthed advances in art, philosophy, science, literature, government, education, philanthropy, and music. There's no Renaissance without our faith. Try making sense of Shakespeare without the Bible. It's the inspiration of our faith that conceived hospitals, orphanages, and universities. The paternity of social justice can be traced to those sixty-six books in the Old and New Testaments. And the list of benefits goes on and on and on.

Don't just take our word for it. In 1948, poet T. S. Eliot wrote:

It is in Christianity that our arts have developed; it is in Christianity that the laws of Europe have—until recently—been rooted. It is against a background of Christianity that all our thought has significance. An individual European may not believe that the Christian Faith is true, and yet what he says, and makes, and does, will all spring out of his heritage of Christian culture and depend on that culture for its meaning. Only a Christian culture could have produced a Voltaire or a Nietzsche. I do not believe that the culture of Europe could survive the complete disappearance of the Christian Faith.

We wholeheartedly agree. So know that we, too, are all-in on righting the ship. Let's get to work!

THE PROBLEM WITH PERCEPTION

Stripped down to its core, Christianity is a *great* product. It's so good that if Christianity were a consumer product, these are some of the promises that would be on its packaging:

- Live forever!
- Get a fresh start!
- Experience unconditional love!
- Your life will have meaning!
- Hope and courage to face the future!
- Your past wrongs wiped out!
- Wake up every day with purpose!
- Experience Forgiveness!
- Have a friend for life!
- No expiration date!
- (And the best part?) It's free!

This line of reasoning might irk some readers, but these miraculous benefits are exactly what Christianity offers to the world.

So the big question is this: *Why isn't the world responding?*

When we started writing this book, we were both convinced that Christianity had a manageable marketing problem. All we had to do was come up with something clever to fix the current negative public perception of Christianity, and then nonbelievers would start responding!

But as it turns out, the real problem isn't marketing at all.

As we will explain in the following chapters, the problem is much worse than we thought.

PART ONE

WHERE DID
WE GO WRONG?

*In many influential cultural, political,
and intellectual precincts,*
C *for* Christian *has become the new scarlet letter.*

MARY EBERSTADT,
IT'S DANGEROUS TO BELIEVE

HOW IN THE WORLD did we get here?

After all, for many people reading this book, we started our school years praying in the classroom, and in those days, it was perfectly normal (especially before exams). Abortion was wrong—no question. Marriage mattered, and it was between a man and a woman. People who would never darken the door of a church still respected it. Phil's father was a pastor in Charlotte, North Carolina, and Jon's was a church music director in Los Angeles, California. In those days, both men were highly regarded by city and business leaders—whether those leaders were Christians or not.

But something happened, and that "something" has turned everything on its head. Today, not only is prayer not welcomed in school, but students have actually been threatened with suspension for attempting it. Abortion on demand is now the law of the land, and no one seems to see the irony in the fact that our culture considers a single cell of *anything* on Mars "life," but on Earth a fetus at eight months isn't. Marriage has pretty much become whatever two consenting adults want it to be, and some have even complained that limiting it to two human beings might be discrimination.

And Christians? In 2017, former presidential candidate Bernie Sanders suggested that Christians are unfit for political office because they are so "hateful."

This was not the world we were born into, and if we're honest, we have to admit the speed and extent of the cultural shift has caught most of us by surprise.

So how did it happen?

How did it all slip away?

CHAPTER 1

SLIPPING AWAY

For increasing millions of people in the wider culture,
Christianity feels like a long list of rules
that matter *to someone else.*

DAVID KINNAMAN AND GABE LYONS,
GOOD FAITH

There's a billboard outside the city limits where I live.
The canvas is white and in large black letters, it reads,
"The fool has said in his heart there is no God."
Nothing else. No relational investment and
no mention of God's immeasurable grace—
just Scripture used to insult nonbelievers.

C. M. JOYNER,
WRITING IN *RELEVANT* MAGAZINE

CHRISTIANS LOVE BEING INFLUENTIAL.

This is not a shocking revelation. Our Christian faith has had a qualitative, positive influence on us, and we want others to experience it too. And with so much wrong out there, with so many people lost and hurting, who can blame us? It's certainly understandable why Christians would want to encourage change in individual lives, in schools, in government, in politics, in culture, in entertainment, and in eternity.

Let's look at the word *influence*. The dictionary defines it as:

1. The capacity or power of persons or things to be a compelling force on or produce effects on the actions, behavior, opinions, etc., of others.
2. A person or thing that exerts influence.

That sounds like us, right? As individuals and as a community, Christians have placed a high priority on influencing the world for the better. So, quick snapshot—how are we doing?

- 75 percent of employees admit to stealing at least once from their employer.
- 60 percent of adults can't have a ten-minute conversation without lying at least once.
- 80 percent of women admit to regularly telling "harmless half-truths."

- 54 percent of marriages now begin with unmarried cohabitation.
- 90 percent of Americans believe infidelity is unacceptable, yet 41 percent of spouses admit to infidelity.
- 68 percent of women and 74 percent of men admit they would have an affair if they knew they would never get caught.
- Last year, there were twenty-one billion visits to adult websites.

If these are the indicators of Christianity's influence on our culture's health, then we're flatlining. What in the world happened? We've got the "good news," and we've got the "path to life"—but it seems that people are less and less interested in hearing our message.

MARKETING THE CHRISTIAN FAITH

The need for marketing our faith began in earnest in the wake of the sexual revolution of the 1960s. Prior to that, churches had for centuries relied on an assumed authority in American culture that didn't require any sort of earnest effort to get people to attend church or pay attention to their message. But by the 1950s, the worrying signs of decades of dry rot were already there.

The early and mid-twentieth century saw the emergence of itinerant revival preachers like Billy Graham and Oral Roberts, who were vastly popular and made a significant impact on American culture.

**People everywhere were in
desperate need of being "revived."
That's because most churches weren't doing the job.**

Once the 1960s hit and questioning authority became acceptable and common, the wheels finally came off, and churches started to lose their implicit right to dictate morality. Marketing to stem the tide became a necessity.

In the ensuing decades, the branding of our faith for the purposes of cultural impact has taken many forms. Most didn't work because they were merely appeals for influence based on the fading-light authority of the church. When the futility of those efforts became painfully obvious, there were "new" awakenings. But really, they were just the same fireworks of influence that tent revivalists have fleetingly lit up the sky with for the last century. That's not to say that many dedicated and committed people haven't worked tirelessly to share the gospel, engage a nonbelieving culture, and work for change. There are churches and Christian organizations doing remarkable work. But any branding that has had, at its root, the goal of restoring Christianity's influence on culture has largely failed.

Need more proof?

- We've protested at major movie studios, and the result? Zero.
- We've boycotted television networks, and the result? Zero.

- We've criticized stores who discourage employees from saying "Merry Christmas," and the result? Zero.
- We've publicized lists of corporations that aren't "faith friendly," and the result? Zero.

We could go on and on, but you get it. An honest and critical look at the last fifty years in America reveals that Christians as a community really haven't moved the dial on *any* moral or cultural issue. Why is that? Why has almost every effort failed?

Maybe it's because we are trying so hard to *influence* people.

INFLUENCE VERSUS EXAMPLE

Wait a minute, you might be thinking. *Aren't Christians supposed to be influencing culture for the better? Shouldn't we influence our friends, neighbors, and coworkers to consider Jesus?* It's a fair question. Regardless of what the answer is, it's critical to understand that, in today's culture, the word *influence* has very negative connotations.

We did an informal survey of nonbelievers we work with in the entertainment industry about what they dislike about Christians. The single biggest response was about influence—*but it wasn't what we expected.* They said things like:

- "Stop telling me how to live my life."
- "I'm sick of Christians trying to push their agenda on me."
- "Don't tell me who I can marry."
- "Just leave me alone."

- "Stop shoving your message down my throat."
- "When did you become the lifestyle cop?"

After that experience, we looked it up in several different sources. Here are a handful of the words that could be used in place of the word *influence*: *Power. Rule. Authority. Bias. Direct. Control. Instigate. Induce. Dominate. Persuade.*

Apparently, the very thing we are trying so hard to do is the thing nonbelievers push back on the most.

When the definition of *influence* includes terms like "a compelling force," "process of producing effects," and "exerts," we can begin to see why the secular world might be repulsed. It's understandable why our good intentions are perceived by outsiders as coercive. We can't just chalk it up to the secular world's hardened hearts. And because of American Christianity's decades-long entanglement in politics, secular people in the United States look at *Christian* influence and fear that we're attempting to impose a biblically based government in America.

This book began with our frustration over how the Christian community has *presented* (or marketed) itself over the last fifty or more years. After all, if "marketing" means presenting your product to the largest audience *and making them desire it*, then by looking at the cultural indicators as a whole, we've done a pretty terrible job. We have to face the fact that much of the time Christians shoot ourselves in the foot by appearing judgmental, indifferent, hypocritical, pushy, and all the others perceptions that pretty much kill a marketing campaign.

Surely we can agree that Jesus was the ultimate Messenger of His own message, right? But when we study the life of Christ, we see something dramatically different.

Jesus didn't seem very concerned about influence.

When Jesus could have been the most influential to the world around Him, He kept unexpectedly pulling back. For instance, after extraordinary acts of healing could have easily made Him a household name, Jesus told the people He had just healed not to tell anyone about Him:

Then Jesus said to him, "See that you don't tell anyone. But go, show yourself to the priest and offer the gift Moses commanded, as a testimony to them." (Matthew 8:4 NIV)

And their eyes were opened. And Jesus sternly warned them, "See that no one knows about it." (Matthew 9:30)

Jesus sternly charged him and sent him away at once, and said to him, "See that you say nothing to anyone, but go, show yourself to the priest and offer for your cleansing what Moses commanded, for a proof to them." (Mark 1:43–44)

Jesus commanded them not to tell anyone. But the more he did so, the more they kept talking about it. (Mark 7:36 NIV)

When the crowds grew to an overwhelming size, and it seemed the perfect moment to expand His influence, Jesus withdrew to be alone:

And those who ate the loaves were five thousand men. Immediately He made his disciples get into the boat and go before Him to the other side, to Bethsaida, while He dismissed the crowd. And after He had taken leave of them, He went up on the mountain to pray. (Mark 6:44–46)

Yet the news about Him spread all the more, so that crowds of people came to hear Him and to be healed of their sicknesses. But Jesus often withdrew to lonely places and prayed. (Luke 5:15–16 NIV)

What, no cameras capturing the moment? No Snapchat or Facebook Live to build up His personal brand? Obviously, Jesus didn't have a very good PR team!

In fact, as the gospel of Mark notes, early in His ministry, it was *demons* who tried to proclaim Jesus to the public. Theologian R. C. Sproul points out that demons were the first to declare His true identity as the Son of God. But it was Jesus Himself who shut them up:

> Now when the sun was setting, all those who had any who were sick with various diseases brought them to Him, and He laid His hands on every one of them and healed them. And demons came out of many, crying, "You are the Son of God!" But He rebuked them and would not allow them to speak, because they knew that He was the Christ. (Luke 4:40–41)

No chance Jesus was clueless about how to influence His culture. No way His actions were unintentional. Maybe He just wasn't concerned with the idea of *influence* at all.

Most incredibly, when His miraculous words and works became widely evident and the crowd expressed a passionate, spontaneous desire for His reign to begin immediately, Jesus bolted:

> After the people saw the sign Jesus performed, they began to say, "Surely this is the Prophet who is to come into the world." Jesus, knowing that they intended to come and make Him king by force, withdrew again to a mountain by himself. (John 6:14–15 NIV)

What was going on? It is clear from the New Testament that, while Jesus never shied away from His message, He was a cautious and calculating Messenger.

We haven't been able to find any real proof that Jesus implemented any of the marketing efforts we've used to try to influence the world around us. There's no evidence that Jesus boycotted anybody, released lists of local companies that weren't friendly to His message, used the Jews' buying power to coerce businesses, or tried to intimidate the Romans into not occupying Israel. He never sought to rally people to divisive political causes or went out of His way to avoid the people He most disagreed with. So maybe it should be no surprise to us that, after decades of those kinds of initiatives, modern Christianity has not only failed to turn things around, but we are actually losing ground.

For most people throughout history, the definition of *influence* is wrapped up in power and control. Whether the influencer intended to use his influence for good or bad, over and over, the perception of those on the receiving end has been about power, corruption, and coercion. Maybe that's why Jesus clearly worked so hard to distance Himself from any action that might be reminiscent of that reality.

When we chase influence, nonbelievers see us as being exactly like them, only with a thin veneer of religiosity. To them, we have the appearance of modern-day Pharisees, so they reject what we're selling. This is exactly why Jesus wasn't interested in *influence* as much as He was interested in *being an example and showing a better way.*

**Maybe the problem with Christianity today
isn't a lack of *influence*.
It's that we're chasing it in the first place.**

If we're being honest, our real concern over our loss of Christianity's influence in today's culture isn't how it reflects on Jesus or His message.

It's that it reflects badly on us.

CHAPTER 2

THE FAT GUY AT THE GYM

We must listen very carefully to the truth
we have heard, or we may drift away from it.

HEBREWS 2:1 NLT

The greatest single cause of atheism in the world today
is Christians who acknowledge Jesus
with their lips and walk out the door and deny Him
by their lifestyle. That is what an unbelieving world
simply finds unbelievable.

NOVELIST BRENNAN MANNING

IN *ANTIGONE*, Sophocles wrote, "None love the messenger who brings bad news," which is the origin of our modern phrase, "Don't shoot the messenger." But if we Christians— Christ's hands and feet on the earth—are even partially responsible for humanity's rejection of the message of Jesus, then "shooting the messenger" may not be such a bad idea.

It can't be our fault, can it? you think. *Not a chance!*

We understand. As we mentioned earlier, when we started this book, we felt the exact same way. As marketing professionals, we were 100 percent certain this was a perception problem, a messaging problem, a branding problem. Now we're convinced otherwise.

Have you ever been to a restaurant where you ask the waiter about a certain menu item, then he shrugs and gives you a less-than-enthusiastic, "It's good"? Do you believe him? If you had a meeting at the Pepsi headquarters and noticed that everyone at the office drank Coke, what would that tell you? If all the mechanics at American Airlines refused to fly in their company's planes, how inclined would you be to buy a ticket?

Well, that's us. Like the people in these examples, we don't believe in our own product.

Christianity doesn't have a marketing problem.
We have a sales force problem.

Study after study from top-quality researchers like Pew, Gallup, and Barna come back with roughly the same numbers again and again. Most adults in this country say they believe in God (89 percent). Only slightly fewer call themselves Christians (70 percent). But what we *say* and what we *do* are two different things.

So to quantify between hyperbole and actual habit, we looked at what should be four common practices of active Christians: *prayer, church attendance, Bible reading,* and *tithing.*

How are Christians doing when it comes to these four essential practices of our faith?

PRAYER

Prayer is the easiest habit of the four to accomplish and the hardest to measure accurately, since prayer includes everything from intercessory prayers of healing with strangers dying in a hospital to a quick, "Dear God, please let me get a parking space at the mall."

On the whole, you'll be pleased to know that:

- 55 percent of Americans pray regularly.

That's good news, right? But here's where the yellow light starts flashing:

- Only 63 percent of *Christians* say prayer is essential. (Pew Research)

Take note: the corollary means that 37 percent of Christians *don't* think prayer is essential. And then there's this little nugget:

- Only 54 percent of people who pray daily attend church every week.

More on that in the next section on church attendance, but again, look at the inversion—that means 46 percent of those who pray daily *don't* attend church weekly. Hmm . . .

CHURCH ATTENDANCE

If we live in a country where 83 percent of Americans identify as "Christian," then how many would you suspect are attending church on a regular basis? It's a trickier question to answer than you might imagine. The first question to ask is, "What defines a regular church attender?" Let's take this out of the church world for a minute.

Consider the nonwork places we all choose to go on a regular basis—the grocery store, the gym, coffee shops, the kids' schools, or restaurants. With most businesses there's no hard-and-fast rule, but a "regular" is someone who stops by often enough to be recognized by the staff or known by name when he or she comes through the door.

In the church world, the rule of thumb now for "regular attender" is three out of eight Sundays. That's right: show up just nineteen Sundays a year, and you're considered a regular!

With that in mind, consider this statistic from Gallup:

- 43 percent of Americans regularly attend church.

When we start to put these numbers together, we realize that only just over half of Americans who identify as a Christian show up to church regularly—*regularly* being defined as around one-third of the time.

In a separate study, the Hartford Institute for Religion Research found that only 20 percent of American Christians are in church weekly. That means 80 percent of American Christians *aren't*.

BIBLE READING

If that last section depressed you, then just wait.

First, the good news. The American Bible Society's annual "State of the Bible" report reveals that the majority of Americans do hold the Bible in high regard. In fact, as many as two-thirds of Americans believe "the Bible contains everything a person needs to know in order to live a meaningful life." According to the study:

- 79 percent believe the Bible is sacred literature.
- 61 percent express a desire to read the Bible more often.

That last stat is fascinating. With billions of Bibles currently in print and free online Bible apps available on every device imaginable, what, exactly, is holding them back from reading it more? Here's where the train really starts to come off the rails:

- Just 36 percent of Americans profess to reading the Bible at least once a week.

It gets worse. LifeWay, which is the retail and research arm of the Southern Baptists, found conclusions even more bleak:

- 19 percent of *churchgoing Christians* read the Bible daily.
- 25 percent of *churchgoing Christians* read the Bible "a few times" a week.
- 40 percent of *churchgoing Christians* read the Bible "once a month, rarely or never."

That last number: ouch! Can you imagine these statistics applying to other fields? Executives who don't care to know the data on their business, car mechanics who don't read manuals, teachers who don't read textbooks, or doctors who rarely consult medical literature?

We would be horrified.

Yet when it comes to the primary book informing us about the God of the universe, His remarkable and unfolding plan for our lives, and our eternal destiny, Christians think so little of it that we read it only when it's convenient.

TITHING

Oh boy, here we go—tithing! You don't even have to read this stat to know it's going to be brutal:

- Fewer than 10 percent of *churchgoers* give 10 percent or more of their income.

Yes, yes, we know—you donate your time, which is *way* more valuable than money, you give to other nonprofits, and so on. (True story—if you hold up this book next to your ear, you can faintly hear the tithing excuses of other people reading it!) But consider this: a pastor in Southern California likes to say, "If you show me how you spend your time and how you spend your money, I'll show you what's important in your life." In light of that and the other previous stats, it's easy to see what's *not* important to us.

Consider the ministry *not* being accomplished locally and around the globe when 90 percent of churchgoers don't tithe—the starving people not fed, the medicine that didn't arrive on time, the water wells not dug, the sexually enslaved not liberated. This lack of tithing investment in our nation's churches is the canary in the coal mine. Our faith is slowly—but surely—choking out.

SUMMARY

Roughly 75 percent of us who identify as Christians aren't attending church with any regularity. Of the ones of us who do, 40 percent aren't reading the Bible at all, and 90 percent aren't tithing anywhere near the level the Bible instructs. We're not talking about fasting or going on mission trips or leading a small group—this is the baseline, common stuff.

Modern Christianity in a nutshell:
All talk, no action.
Big hat, no cattle.

It's a safe assumption that if you're reading a book about how to fix what ails modern Christianity, then you care about the state of the church. Maybe in these stats you were convicted by your own haphazard and lethargic devotion to these basic spiritual practices. (The numbers don't lie—that's most of us.) Maybe as you have been reading this, you have been building a rampart of defensive excuses. (Yep, that's us too.) But perhaps you find yourself in the ever-dwindling camp of frequent church attenders, Bible readers, active prayers, and faithful tithers. Maybe you're one of the hearty few who is an every-weeker at church, who is up and reading a devotional before dawn, and who is tithing 10 percent on the gross.

Even if that's the case, you must understand how damaging these stats are to you, your daily ministry, and your church. Confronted with the realities of our gross dereliction to the outward proof of our faith, those adjectives that non-Christians use to describe our community—*hypocritical, phony, judgmental, insensitive*—suddenly stick.

All of us get tarred with the same brush.

One of the common criticisms Jesus faced was that He spent too much time with sinners. He associated with the unwelcomed and unappreciated of society. How many of us could be accused of spending too much time with the "riff raff?"

—MISSIOLOGIST AND RESEARCHER ED STETZER

To the outside world, we've become the fat guy in the gym who's lecturing everyone else about health. We're the shameless politician who campaigns to raise taxes but who doesn't pay them himself. We're the celebrity who preaches about the dangers of global warming but flies everywhere in a gas-guzzling private jet.

All talk, no action.

It's no wonder the culture isn't interested. If our actions essentially tell the world that we don't believe in the product *ourselves*, then why should they? To put it in advertising terms, by not being remotely committed as a community to the gospel we preach, Christians have damaged our own brand in the eyes of the public.

There's no point in wasting any more time with tweaking our messaging. The issue is far more sinister and deadly than that. Like a high school football coach, we need to stop and study the game films. If we're ever going to find our way back, then for our sake—and theirs—we need to figure out the root of where we've gone wrong.

CHAPTER 3

THAT OTHER GOD

The inattentive, slovenly way we drift
into the presence of God is an indication
that we are not bothering to think about Him.

OSWALD CHAMBERS,
MORAL FOUNDATIONS OF LIFE

The only way to avoid the true God is to fabricate
a false god that's controllable.

PASTOR TIMOTHY KELLER

REMEMBER THE GOOD OLD DAYS?

In his writings, C. S. Lewis often referenced the German term *sehnsucht*. It's a word that is almost impossible to translate to English, but all of us have experienced it.

Have you ever been back to your childhood home? In your memory, the house was so big and the neighborhood oh-so-treelined and idyllic! Only now you discover the house is actually tiny and the street kind of a dump. Or what about that *amazing* restaurant you went to on your first date? Remember how delicious the food was? Only now that you go back, you think, *Wow, this food is awful.* That's *sehnsucht.* It's the longing or yearning for something that was probably more imagined than real.

Sehnsucht seems appropriate in the context of our fading Christian culture. When Christians look back on those golden days that keep receding into the distance, we like to imagine that it's the world that walked away from our influence. But the harsh truth is that it's Christians who have done the walking away.

**We have abandoned our faith.
We're just the last to notice.**

The first two chapters of this book dealt with Christians' loss of influence in our culture and placed the blame squarely where it belongs: on us—for unwisely chasing influence in the first place. In this chapter, we hope to wrap our hands around the root problem and yank it out of the parched landscape of our once-vibrant faith. (That's Phil's PhD talking right there.)

In any quest to encounter the true God, believers will encounter crises and challenges and crossroads all along the journey. *Sanctification*, the fifty-cent theological word derived from two Latin words meaning "to make holy," is the journey from who we once were to who we will be in eternity. It's an arduous, lifelong process. Saints aren't made in a day. In theory, the closer we get to sanctification or "holiness," the more our failings should grieve us.

But hundreds of millions of us have abandoned the narrow road that leads to Christlikeness. Instead, we've ventured off in another direction to a vast, glistening boulevard. Wide and easy is this road, and in the distance, we are beckoned into the presence of another deity. Here is our present-day spiritual home. We find ourselves standing in awe at the temple of That Other God.

It's easy to see why millions of fellow travelers have stopped and remained here. That Other God is incredible! Loving, forgiving, kind, and supportive, That Other God understands where we've been and where we want to go. That Other God isn't vengeful, and he graciously overlooks our weaknesses. That Other God is a faithful and nonjudgmental friend who offers us acceptance and approval and expects only our love in return. That Other God knows that our intentions are pure, even if our actions prove otherwise. In short, That Other God is all the things we want and none of the stuff we don't.

Who is this wonderful deity we now worship?

That Other God is *you*.
That Other God is *me*.

In Genesis 1:27, God made humanity "in his own image." But modern believers have inverted this, and we have now made a god in *our* own image. This god of our making doesn't mind if we infrequently attend church, never study His Word, pray to Him only with our laundry list of self-absorbed desires, and only occasionally throw a few spare bucks His way. "You're welcome, God" is now our heart's cry.

That Other God now so dominates our spiritual horizon that the traditional expectations of the God of the Bible now seem excessive, capricious, onerous, and possibly evil. Keeping the Sabbath, fasting, believing hell is a real place, practicing self-denial, sharing the gospel, serving those less fortunate than ourselves, and suffering in any way—these arcane principles are as out-of-fashion as mullets and shoulder pads. That Other God not only shuns such old-fashioned nonsense but sneers at those who dare attempt to burden others with this outmoded morality. That Other God rejects the clear standards of what a transformed Christian life should be.

Because that's how we like it.

In the ancient world, men and women would make art to

influence hoped-for outcomes, such as symbols for fertility, talismans for good luck, and carvings to encourage a bountiful harvest. Since these results were beyond their scope of control, people created these sculptures and icons to better their chances of success by bringing the spiritual realm onto their side.

They were called idols.

Modern readers of the Bible quickly skim past the ancient warnings against idol worship, thinking they have little relevance anymore. But should we so casually dismiss these verses? The sin of idolatry was that people created their own idols and imbued them with power. God railed against these imperfect, man-made, self-serving versions of Him.

Sounds a lot like us.

THAT OTHER GOD IS *OUR* IDOL

As Christians, we all must test our own faith in the light of such an accusation. Like the ancients, modern Christians have created That Other God out of our self-serving expectations for the Almighty.

Consider your own spiritual journey. How much do your wants and demands determine your relationship with God? Do you approach the Creator of the universe on His terms or yours? What commandments, verses, and instructions do you consider to be no longer relevant to your contemporary lifestyle? Have you conformed your worldview to God's, or have your ideas of who you think God should be modified His worldview to conform to your own?

The apostle John wrote, "Dear children, keep away from

anything that might take God's place in your hearts" (1 John 5:21 NLT). This wise admonishment was written by a man who spent a lifetime watching people rise and fall on their journey with Christ. Of course, today's Christians are not the first generation of Jesus followers to veer off course. But because of our selfie culture, we have taken idolatry to an impressive new level. The brilliance of That Other God is that this made-up version looks, smells, and tastes just like God, but it is a forgery.

We speak not as accusers here, but as humbled coconspirators. The realization that we, too have substituted That Other God in place of the one true God in many areas of our lives has caused anguished soul-searching in both of us. How many years has our faith been a golden-calf version of ourselves painted with a thin veneer of Holy Spirit to make it outwardly presentable to our fellow Christians? How long have we chased the Sunday "feeling" of being in the presence of God because it's more convenient than doing the hard work of being in the presence of God every day?

**Working out is hard.
But wearing yoga pants is easy.**

We feel so strongly about this that we almost titled the book *That Other God.*

When you read the Bible, you see how often—even after God does amazing things for His people—they turn back to That Other God. They do it because it's so much easier to worship a God of our own making than it is to worship the true God. And every time the people worshiped That Other God, terrible things eventually happened. So they cried out to God again, and the cycle started all over. And over and over and over.

To see a compressed version of that cycle, reread the story of King Nebuchadnezzar starting in the second chapter of the book of Daniel. Man, that guy just didn't get it . . . but the truth is, he's a lot like us.

Even within generations with people who had actually seen the real God do amazing things (multiple times), once the people got fat and happy, they deferred to the easier God they made up.

That's exactly what is happening today—and why Christians are making so little impact in our culture. We begin to justify our lack of holiness and think things like, *That Other God doesn't care if I miss church. He's much nicer, has no requirements for outdated things like holiness, and understands my affair because he knows my wife is boring, because after all, it's all about acceptance, right?*

Whenever we talk to Christians today about social issues, we hardly ever hear them quote the Bible. Instead, they usually start their answers with, "Well, for *me*, I think . . ."

One of our friends is pastor Joe Champion at Celebration Church near Austin. At his staff meetings, when a team member pitches a new idea for a church outreach, event, or leadership issue, Joe simply says, "What does the Scripture say about that?" And if they can't support their idea from Scripture, they drop it and move on.

What if we lived our lives that way?

Sadly, for decades, our churches have unconsciously allowed That Other God to block the way to the altar of the Lord. Just think of all of the sermon topics that pastors now won't dare touch!

In truth, most of these decisions to allow an idol in our midst were reactions to the loss of Christian influence in society. For example, what makes you a Christian in many churches nowadays? It's pretty simple, actually. Just say the "sinner's prayer" for the assurance of eternity . . . and that's the whole ball game. For many churches, that's where obedience ends, and no one who steps through the door is encouraged past that point.

We are now seeing the unintended consequences of setting the bar so low. First, there is little to no evidence of transformed lives in our congregations. Sure, there are a handful of great testimonies in every house of worship (probably from the pool of the 20 percent who are still showing up weekly). But when precious few are seeing tangible differences in their own hearts, when even fewer of their fellow attendees remind them of the heroic characters in the Bible, and when genuine miracles are nowhere to be found, discouraged churchgoers walk away more disillusioned than if we had kept the bar high in the first place.

Does your church prioritize pushing you hard—like a relentlessly encouraging personal trainer for your soul—into a deeper and more profound relationship with Christ? Or do they—like a rose-scented convalescent hospital—specialize in keeping you warm, dry, and comfortable? Odds are, it's probably the latter. In his book *The Pursuit of God*, A. W. Tozer wrote of our churches, "It is a solemn thing, and no small scandal in the Kingdom, to see God's children starving while actually seated at the Father's table." That was written in 1947—how much worse is it now?

Our secret devotion to That Other God is nothing new. Adam's original sin was wanting things his own way too. Adam wasn't alone. The Bible is filled with stories of men and women who were willing to follow God—but only on their own terms. Abraham's sexual tryst with Sarah's maid, Jonah's attempted escape from his assignment in Nineveh, Samson's, David's, and Solomon's spectacular falls from grace, the rich young ruler, Judas—each story ends in tragedy. They serve as a warning to us to stop dead in our tracks and take the way back to a vibrant faith.

But how do we correct a problem that dates back to Adam? How do we keep ourselves from diverting off the path again? How do we fix our churches so that they don't keep leading us into low expectations? Finally, how do we heal the damage we have done to the brand of Christianity?

To answer these questions, we must go back two thousand years.

PART TWO

WHEN THE DAWN IS STILL DARK

Pure and undefiled religion before God and the Father
is this: to visit orphans and widows in their trouble,
and to keep oneself unspotted from the world.

JAMES 1:27 NKJV

ONE MIGHT ASSUME, based on the conclusions in Part One, that we have a negative view of the future of the church. After all, we've proposed that the primary reason for the decline in Christianity's influence in America and around the globe should be laid entirely at our feet—nonbelievers are no longer moved or inspired by most modern Christians because we worship a false idol, a god cast in our own image that we've deluded ourselves into thinking is the real God. (Well, when you put it like *that*, it does sound pretty grim . . .)

And while the trend line is definitely headed in the wrong direction, there is hope.

"So," as Jim Carrey's character famously said in *Dumb and Dumber*, "You're telling me there's a chance?!"

More than a chance! We believe that, with a renewed commitment to the original message of Jesus Christ by our community, the best days of the church are ahead of it, not behind it. We believe that there are still billions of lives ready to join the great and celebratory cloud of witnesses, and that we on Jesus's team have a critical role to play in packing that party out.

With the ever-evolving world of media platforms, global connectivity, and technological marvels, there are now immeasurable opportunities to share the gospel in ingenious and inventive ways. Beyond the horizon, there are innumerable lives that will be transformed in ways we've not even yet begun to imagine. Despite our present circumstances, we believe our best days are yet to come.

Hope begins in the dark, the stubborn hope that if you just show up and try to do the right thing, the dawn will come. You wait and watch and work: you don't give up.

—ANNE LAMOTT, *BIRD BY BIRD*

But before the dawn, we must arise from our warm and complacent bed, pull on our sweats, put on our trainers, and head out into the cold.

It's time for us, as Navy SEALs like to say, to get, "wet and sandy."

CHAPTER 4

"THIS IS A FOOTBALL"

If we were left to ourselves with the task of taking
the gospel to the world, we would immediately
begin planning innovative strategies and plotting
elaborate schemes. We would organize conventions,
develop programs, and create foundations. . . .
But Jesus is so different from us. With the task of taking
the gospel to the world, he wandered through
the streets and byways. . . . All He wanted was
a few men who would think as he did, love as he did,
see as he did, teach as he did, and serve as he did.
All He needed was to revolutionize the hearts of a few,
and they would impact the world.

DAVID PLATT,
RADICAL

One of the paradoxes of history is the relationship
between the beliefs and the practices
of the early Christians as compared to those
of the culture around them.

TIMOTHY KELLER,
THE REASON FOR GOD

THEY HAD NOTHING.

No money. No political power. No organizational skills. No education. No experience. No plan whatsoever. As a matter of fact, after Jesus ascended from the Mount of Olives into the brilliant sky, His disciples stood there with their mouths wide open.

Two angels were needed to give them a nudge:

> While they were gazing into heaven as he went, behold, two men stood by them in white robes, and said, "Men of Galilee, why do you stand looking into heaven? This Jesus, who was taken up from you into heaven, will come in the same way as you saw him go into heaven." (Acts 1:10–11)

What must have been the conversation on the day's journey back to Jerusalem? Unfortunately, the Bible doesn't tell us— some details in Scripture are undoubtedly left to our imagination by design. We suspect one of the disciples sheepishly said, "Okay, so, now what do we do?"

They had nothing.

But they must have done something right. Fast-forward a few hundred years, and Christianity had become the prime mover in the Western world.

But how? How did an unorganized, ostracized, persecuted, ragtag group started by a bunch of illiterate fishermen that was, at most, considered an obscure Jewish sect in a backwater province eventually become the official religion of the Roman Empire?

BACK TO THE BEGINNING

One of the greatest leaders in the history of sports was Green Bay Packers Football Coach Vince Lombardi. During the 1960s, Lombardi won five championships in seven years, and he won the first two Super Bowls ever played. In the pantheon of NFL coaches, he is considered one of the best, the cream of the crop.

But for all of his brilliant decisions in the heat of football games, one of his greatest moments was in 1961 as the Green Bay Packers football team gathered around him on the first day of training camp. The previous season, the Packers had gone all the way to the top—only to lose unexpectedly to the Philadelphia Eagles in the NFL Championship Game.

When they began the next season, the Packers were the second-best team in the league. The team was comprised of seasoned professionals—experts at the game. After enduring such a heartbreaking loss at the end of the last season, they had all arrived at camp ready to move to the next level and win a championship of their own.

But Coach Lombardi had a surprise up his sleeve.

In his brilliantly written book, *When Pride Still Mattered: A Life of Vince Lombardi,* author David Maraniss explains:

He took nothing for granted. He began a tradition of starting from scratch, assuming that the players were blank slates who carried over no knowledge from the year before. . . . He began with the most elemental statement of all. "Gentlemen," he said, holding a pigskin in his right hand, "this is a football."

Some of his players were stunned, and others thought it was a joke. These were men who had excelled at college football, spent years at the professional level, and were at the top of their game. Lombardi's statement was demeaning and probably offensive for players at that level. But he knew that to achieve greatness, they needed to go back to the very beginning.

Even if our heartfelt desire is to walk away from That Other God (and that is a critically important step), the allure of this idol is strong. It will take much more than willpower. To walk away once and for all from a god we built to suit ourselves will take serious relearning. We have veered miles off course from Jesus's original vision for His church.

For Christians to get back to the beginning, we must first understand what the world of the Early Church was really like.

Only with that understanding can we fully appreciate the radically different worldview and lifestyle of the first believers— and then begin to emulate it ourselves.

At this point, it may be worth mentioning that six months after Coach Lombardi's "This is a football" meeting about getting back to the fundamentals, the Green Bay Packers went on to beat the New York Giants 37–0 to win the NFL Championship. Perhaps it's time for us to get back to the basics as well.

A TWO-THOUSAND-YEAR-OLD STRATEGY
FOR ENGAGING CULTURE
WITH THE CHRISTIAN FAITH

The Christian writer and theologian Tatian was a Syrian who lived in the second century. Born in Assyria (Mesopotamia), he later journeyed to Rome, where he discovered Christianity. He was shocked at the pagan cults he saw throughout the city and began reflecting on religious issues. During his investigation, he read the Old Testament—and the more he read, the more he realized just how unreasonable paganism was. As a result, he decided to become a Christian.

Tatian's "Address to the Greeks," written about AD 170, tells the story of his conversion. This account is so compelling that we immediately thought it a model for how we can engage the secular culture of today—two thousand years after Tatian. Here's his story:

I withdrew myself and sought best how to discover the truth. While I was earnestly employed in this matter, I happened to light upon certain 'barbaric' (non-Greek) writings, too old to be compared with the opinions of the Greeks and too divine to be compared with their error. I found myself convinced by these writings, because of the unpretentious cast of the language, the unstudied character of the writers, the ready comprehension of the making of the universe, the foreknowledge of things to come, the excellence of the precepts and the placing of all things under the rule of one principle. My soul being thus taught by God, I understood that the pagan writings led to condemnation, whereas these put an end to the slavery that is in the world, rescuing us from many rulers, yes, from ten thousand tyrants. These writings do not indeed give us something which we had not received before but rather something which we had indeed received but were prevented by error from making our own.

Let's review his revelation about reading the Scriptures and consider how we could use the same ideas to engage today's culture. Tatian said that he became convinced of the reality of the Christian faith because of these things:

- *The unpretentious language.* Though Tatian was a learned man, he wasn't moved by an overly academic approach. He was moved by the sincere and unpretentious attitude of the Scripture.
- *The unstudied character of the writers.* God didn't choose the most brilliant people to write the Old Testament; He chose the most willing.
- *The ready comprehension of the universe.* The gospel is a unified vision of how and why we exist.
- *The foreknowledge of things to come.* The Bible didn't leave us hanging. It points to a greater future.

- *The excellence of the precepts.* He couldn't argue with the logic and excellence of the Bible's principles.
- *The unity of principle.* Scripture placed everything under one principle—a unified vision. The Old Testament he was reading was pointing to Jesus.

Perhaps most importantly was this: pagan writings led to condemnation, but Christian writings put an end to the slavery that was in the world.

Think about each of these principles as you engage today's culture with the gospel. Are you pointing them to these same signposts that Tatian saw back in AD 170?

After two thousand years, I'm not sure there's a better model for presenting the truth of the Christian message to nonbelievers.

When it comes to engaging our culture with the Christian faith, *this* is our "football."

CHAPTER 5

THE LINE THAT NEVER ENDED

The New Testament church was birthed in a cultural
and political cesspool. There were no family values.
Sexual perversion was normative, human life cheap,
and justice nonexistent for anyone except the rich
and powerful. . . . Yet none of the New Testament
letters say anything about what we could call
culture warfare. And the passages that deal
with spiritual warfare are always framed in the context
of personal spirituality and righteousness.

LARRY OSBORNE,
MISSION CREEP

Christianity is like a nail.
The harder you strike it, the deeper it goes.

YEMELYAN YAROSLAVSKY,
CHAIRMAN OF STALIN'S LEAGUE
OF THE MILITANT GODLESS IN 1921

PUBLIC PERCEPTION BEGINS to change when other people see that you are serious. For the Early Church, their commitment to the gospel could not be deterred.

To the modern Western mind-set, observing life in the ancient world is an extraordinary combination of foreign and familiar. Some aspects—like pervasive sexuality and government taxation—sound familiar to our own culture. However, other traits—like desperate poverty and ubiquitous slavery—seem foreign to our enlightened and progressive worldviews. Daily life for Christians falls into the latter category.

"The Way" (as the Christian faith was often called back then) grew after the death and resurrection of Jesus, but that growth came at a serious price. Larry Hurtado, in his book *Destroyer of the Gods: Early Christian Distinctiveness in the Roman World*, says, "In the eyes of many of that time, early Christianity was odd, bizarre, and in some ways even dangerous." (Does that sound a bit like how the culture views us today?)

At best, the early followers of Jesus were tolerated by society, who considered them members of an odd Jewish-like cult. At worst, Christians were outcasts who were regularly arrested, jailed, beaten, or killed depending on the mood of the angry mob and/or the local authorities.

For the Early Church, persecution was a way of life.

If you were a follower of Jesus, the threat of being arrested and killed was a common experience and a consideration wherever you went. And economic or political status in society did not provide much safe haven either. For example, the Roman emperor Domitian not only murdered believers, but he did it even when those believers were members of his own family. In *The Triumph of Christianity,* sociologist and historian Rodney Stark reports that ordinary Christians were also seized, "including harmless elderly women such as Apollonia of Alexandria, who had all of her remaining teeth smashed out before being burned alive."

And let's make no mistake about the brutality of Roman persecution. When officials needed a scapegoat, Christians were hunted down for arrest, torture, and death. Many believe that Nero deceptively blamed the great fire of Rome on Christians and inflicted savage tortures on that community. Some scholars believe the apostle Peter may have been one of his victims.

Historians believe many of these arrests were made to acquire victims for sport in the arena. The "Super Bowl" of the time in Rome was the Colosseum—a place where human beings were ripped apart and devoured by wild animals for the amusement of the general public. Stark called the Colosseum a place "worthy of a boy's birthday treat," since people of the time considered it suitable for family entertainment. While Christians who happened to be Roman citizens were exempted from being fed to animals for public amusement, others were not and suffered brutally.

This was more than a gruesome spectacle, however. The goal of these public tortures and murders was to snuff out this potentially dangerous cult and discourage others from joining. Roman authorities assumed that public shaming and executions would put a stop to what they considered to be foolishness about this Jewish teacher named Jesus.

To make the necessary example, the church fathers were typically chosen first. But to the surprise of the Roman authorities, the line of the willing grew. Once a bishop was murdered, a priest would step forward. Once that priest was executed, a local deacon would volunteer. Behind that deacon stood a long line of believers ready to meet their death rather than recant or denounce the name of Jesus.

In fact, the numbers were so great that church fathers had to forbid voluntary martyrdom. But in spite of those well-meaning decrees, surviving documents report a very large number of men and women who still *volunteered* to be martyrs for their faith. While there's no question that some denied their faith or renounced Jesus of Nazareth, there's also no question that most stood in the face of agonizing torture and boldly stared it down.

> How could mere mortals remain defiant after being skinned and covered with salt? How could anyone keep the faith while being slowly roasted on a spit? Such performances seemed virtually supernatural in and of themselves. And that was the effect they often had on the observers.
>
> —RODNEY STARK, *THE TRIUMPH OF CHRISTIANITY*

Through it all, these early believers held fast. Their remarkable and unrelenting commitment to the faith gave Christianity a credibility that transformed their perception in the eyes of the Romans.

And perception did its work. Ancient accounts report that the impact these martyrs had on nonbelievers was powerful and compelling. After all, the Romans weren't prepared to suffer like this for their gods, so who were these people, and who was this god they served? Those questions had to be answered. Rome was the most powerful empire on the planet—but when it came to unwavering commitment, the Roman authorities had met their match.

> Perhaps above all else, Christianity bought a new conception of humanity to a world saturated with capricious cruelty and the vicarious love of death.
>
> —RODNEY STARK, *THE RISE OF CHRISTIANITY*

In such a punishing environment, where these (mostly) new believers were being hunted and killed, they had every right to run for their lives. To flee, recant, or denounce their faith would be entirely understandable. But Christians astonished the ancient world with their radical perspective on humanity. In spite of public persecutions, Christians would press deeper into societal problems, such as moving into the most intense areas of the plague to minister to those infected. In fact, Dionysius, an early bishop, wrote a tribute about the nursing skill of fellow Christians:

Heedless of danger, they took charge of the sick, attending to their every need and ministering to them in Christ, and with them departed this life serenely happy; for they were infected by others with the disease, drawing on themselves the sickness of their neighbors and cheerfully accepting their pains. Many, in nursing and curing others, transferred their death to themselves and died in their stead . . .

Dionysius also wrote about the reaction of those outside the Christian community to the plague:

The heathens behaved in the very opposite way. At the first onset of the disease, they pushed the sufferers away and fled from their dearest, throwing them into the roads before they were dead and treated unburied corpses as dirt, hoping thereby to avert the spread and contagion of the fatal disease; but do what they might, they found it difficult to escape.

The difference in the reaction to the plague was a shock to the Romans, and they found it unfathomable and difficult to process. But there were plenty more ways these early Christians left a profound mark on their world, such as:

- Elevating the role of women in the culture
- Refusing to have abortions
- Valuing female children as much as males

- Men loving and caring for their wives, and not pursing sex outside of marriage
- Experiencing joy even in persecution
- Committing to help the poor and needy
- Taking care of widows and orphans
- Pooling their meager possessions to share with those in need

As the list grew, their impact on the culture grew. Eventually, Christians could not be dismissed or ignored. Perhaps just as important, they were consistent. These issues weren't a fad, trend, or short-term "evangelistic campaign"—this was the way they consistently lived their lives.

THE DEATH OF INFANTICIDE

Abandoning newborns to die of exposure—either on or outside the walls of the city—was a normal part of Roman life. It's what you did if you had an unwanted child, if it was a female or a bastard, if it was weak or sickly, or if it was simply a mouth you couldn't or wouldn't feed. "Exposure" was such a commonly accepted practice across Rome and Greece that people rarely gave it a second thought.

In his book *When Children Became People: The Birth of Childhood in Early Christianity,* historian O. M. Bakke discovered that in ancient Rome, infants were not even named until eight to ten days after birth. The likelihood that they would be killed or left to die of exposure was so high that there was no point in even naming them until a parent had decided their fate.

The Early Church was opposed to infanticide because they believed each person was made in the image of God. However, as a persecuted minority, Christians were in no position to force political change or even to speak out against infanticide to the greater culture. But with such a moral atrocity common throughout the Roman Empire, they had to do something.

They couldn't *fight*, but they could *be*.

First, believers began by outlawing the practice of infanticide among themselves. Moral credibility matters. So the Early Church started with their own people first—and the principle wasn't optional. They started inside the church and worked out.

Second, under the dark of night, these apparently "crazy" people who identified themselves with the teachings of Jesus would go out to the city walls, rescue abandoned babies, take them into their families, and raise them as their own. They did it because it's what Jesus would have done.

Their behavior was baffling to the Romans.

Not only would Christians raise these abandoned children in their own families, but the church community would pitch in the funds to help families pay the expenses of additional children. The Romans had no context for that kind of behavior. It couldn't be explained, and eventually, it made an impact on the culture. Some historians believe that, although infanticide had been a part of the ancient Roman and Greek worlds for hundreds of years, it was how these early Christians responded that began to alter attitudes.

To the Romans, the Christian community's lifestyle difference became more and more apparent. Rodney Stark writes in *The Triumph of Christianity*, "In fact, devout Christian married couples may have had sex more often than did the average pagan couple, because brides were more mature when they married and because husbands were less likely to take up with other women."

Because of such glaring differences, the Early Church's proactively positive response to Roman norms—like prohibiting the practice of child brides, banning abortion, and raising women to higher positions of authority and power—slowly began to change the empire. And as the Roman world started to shift its attitudes toward Christians, these early believers quietly gained more access and made a greater impact.

Much of Christian history has been lived this way, like it was during the Roman Empire, when a small number of Christians modeled another way to live. In a culture like ours, we need to demonstrate first how faith in Christ makes a difference in how we live.

—PHILIP YANCEY, *VANISHING GRACE*

The Early Church's decisions were likely made based on questions the Romans wrestled with themselves. For instance, unwanted children were a problem for Roman families with limited incomes. Even though an abortion in ancient times was a grisly procedure, it seemed the only way out—particularly in a patriarchal culture where the husband had total control over his wife.

But without preaching, arrogance, or condescension, Christians offered a better way.

When the plague hit, the average Roman saw his or her leaders run for their lives to their country estates because it was every man for himself. But Christians loved each other. They helped those in need. Even at the risk of their own lives, they went to the places where the disease was at its worst— so much so that historian Rodney Stark says, "Disease helped Christianity conquer Rome."

Without confrontation, protest, or debate, love did its work.

Why did the Early Church succeed where we are failing? How did they transform the Western world in such a relatively short time? They did things that baffled the Romans. The Early Church didn't picket, they didn't boycott, and they didn't gripe about what was going on in their culture. They just did things that astonished the Romans. They took in abandoned babies. They helped the sick and wounded. They restored dignity to the slaves. They were willing to die for what they believed. After a while, their actions so softened the hearts of the Romans that the Romans wanted to know more about who these Christians were and who was the God they represented.

The question is—what could our Christian community do today that would so astonish nonbelievers that they would be forced to reexamine what we believe and why we believe it?

What would so grab the attention of our culture in a positive way that it would be talked about in homes, in the workplace, and in the mainstream media? In a culture driven by media buzz, what could Christians do that nonbelievers would start talking about?

In Acts 17, the apostle Paul connected with intellectual elites at Mars Hill:

Paul, standing in the midst of the Areopagus, said: "Men of Athens, I perceive that in every way you are very religious. For as I passed along and observed the objects of your worship, I found also an altar with this inscription: 'To the unknown god.' What therefore you worship as unknown, this I proclaim to you. The God who made the world and everything in it, being Lord of heaven and earth, does not live in temples made by man, nor is he served by human hands, as though he needed anything, since he himself gives to all mankind life and breath and everything. And he made from one man every nation of mankind to live on all the face of the earth, having determined allotted periods and the boundaries of their dwelling place, that they should seek God, and perhaps feel their way toward him and find him. Yet he is actually not far from each one of us, for

"'In him we live and move and have our being';
as even some of your own poets have said,
"'For we are indeed his offspring.'

Being then God's offspring, we ought not to think that the divine being is like gold or silver or stone, an image formed by the art and imagination of man. The times of ignorance God overlooked, but now he commands all people everywhere to repent, because he has fixed a day on which he will judge the world in righteousness by a man whom he has appointed; and of this he has given assurance to all by raising him from the dead."

Now when they heard of the resurrection of the dead, some mocked. But others said, "We will hear you again about this." (Acts 17:22–32)

Notice that Paul connected with the intellectual elites of his day on the basis of what *they* thought was important. He didn't begin the conversation talking about what was important to *him*; he started by talking about what was important to *them*. In addition, it's important to remember that while Paul spoke to these influencers from a biblical perspective, *not once* did he quote Scripture.

Paul's decision to engage these philosophers on Mars Hill was significant because this was a public volley. In other words, Paul felt it was time to move beyond the religious community and engage with the leading philosophical thinkers of his day. Certainly, it would have been far easier to stay in the bubble of people who already believed, but he was willing to step out because he knew Christianity could compete in the marketplace of ideas.

Using that as a template, what are the issues of importance to today's society—and your local community—that if we addressed them fully and from the perspective of the gospel, people would be forced to rethink who we are and the God we serve?

Eventually, the emperor Constantine came to power, professed Christianity, and launched a massive church building campaign across the Roman Empire. Christianity dominated the Roman world and grew across all of Europe and the West. But that shift began not because of military power, governmental decree, economic pressure, or civil authority. It began because Christians acted decisively on what they believed within their own community, and people noticed.

Writing in *Christianity Today*, Daniel Yang recognized the link between the impact of the Early Church and today:

> If there was ever a Golden Age of religion, it had to be the first century when the New Testament Church was birthed in the messiness of a religiously pluralistic society. When theology was born out of necessity for survival rather than academics and scholarly debate. When epistles were sent out to nourish fledgling churches with fresh apostolic insights about Messiah

King Jesus who had already come and would come again.

Modern-day Evangelicals aren't equipped to feel comfortable in this space. We're not used to seeing devotees of other religions—or non-religions for that matter—that are just as loud and just as convinced as we are. But, historically, this is the space that Christianity as a movement has felt most comfortable and has shined the brightest.

If this model of living sounds foreign to the practice of your contemporary walk with Jesus, then you're not alone. Such dangerous faith is rarely taught from our pulpits or encouraged in our churches. Modern Christians in the West simply don't live this way.

Because what the Early Church believed in is totally different than what we believe in now.

CHAPTER 6

THE S^7 MYSTERIES

Something is wrong when our lives
make sense to unbelievers.

FRANCIS CHAN,
CRAZY LOVE

WARNING: This chapter contains math.
(We apologize in advance.)

REMEMBER YOUR DAYS in geometry? Did you have a teacher who diagrammed what a difference a degree makes the farther you get from the origination point? Here's an example: if you were traveling toward a specific destination and were off by a single degree—after one foot you'd be off course by only 0.2 inches. Hardly even noticeable to the naked eye, right?

But what happens when you travel a longer distance?

After a mile, you'd be off target by 92 feet. Traveling from your town by circumnavigating around the globe, you'd miss coming back to your current location by more than 435 miles. Oops. And if you were traveling from the earth to the sun in a straight line, you'd be off by 1.6 million miles!

The same is true for our faith. Standing a few feet from the origination point, our modern Christian beliefs don't seem all that different than those of the Early Church. But the longer we've lingered at the temple of That Other God, the more distant our beliefs have become from those of the first believers. That ever-growing chasm is most evident in the Bible verses we choose to ignore as a community. An example of this is Matthew 19:23–24: "Truly I say to you, only with difficulty will a rich person enter the kingdom of heaven. Again I tell you, it is easier for a camel to go through the eye of a needle than for a rich person to enter the kingdom of God."

That's pretty clear—Jesus even repeated Himself so there would be no confusion. But the widening distance between our present condition (America is the richest and fattest country in the history of humanity) and Jesus's unambiguous statements forces us into either making a tortured analysis of the prose— "Oh, it's just a metaphor. See, the 'eye of the needle' is actually a gate outside of Jerusalem . . ."—or ignoring this statement altogether. For example, when most pastors preach the Beatitudes, they use Matthew's version, "Blessed are the poor in spirit," over Luke's version, "Blessed are you who are poor." That way, there are fewer angry post-sermon emails.

But the further this separation grows, the less plausible it seems that we moderns could ever possess the same radically trusting faith that the Early Church had. When we stop teaching these unrealistic and uncomfortable verses, we give insufficient data points to believers to figure out our faith's complex equations. And the inability to land on the right answer only causes more frustration and doubt, which leads to a further contraction of our willingness to step out in trust. It becomes a vicious circle (sorry, more math).

But the rock-hard faith of the Early Church—the fortitude that stood strong in the face of persecution, the trusting commitment to pick up abandoned children and love them as your own, the unwavering confidence to believe in miracles even while burning at the stake—*this* is where we are meant to be living every minute of every day.

Somewhere along the way, we stopped aiming for radically impossible God-sized dreams and instead settled for realistically incremental man-sized progress.

That's why the modern church has become fixated on leadership building, worship debates, organizational structure, church networks, the hip factor, social media, and other easily controllable strategies. There's nothing wrong with many of these techniques, but none is a sufficient replacement for the primary reason churches exist: *the transformation of people's hearts*. Until the church as a whole is chasing dreams that are impossible without God, we are always going to be receding.

Every other religious faith wants to *escape* the world,
but Jesus wants us to *renew* the world.
That must start with a renewal of ourselves.

In the previous chapter, we looked at different ways the Early Church caused the surrounding culture to reconsider who Christians were and the God they served. But we wanted to look even closer—to try and uncover early believers' core beliefs and practices that caused to them to arrive at such a different destination than modern believers. What we found was so profound that it reoriented how we now live out our daily faith.

We discovered seven mysteries that Early Church attendees were *radically committed to*—areas that most modern churches no longer make a priority. Today, there are a million books on "Christian living" that outline attitudes and behaviors that make us look more like Jesus. But we were looking for the mostly abandoned practices that historically caused others to see Jesus in believers and start asking questions for themselves.

These seven areas are:

- Surrender
- Scripture
- Submission
- Service
- Sacrifice
- Simplicity
- Suffering

We call these practices the S^7 Mysteries. To understand the fundamental power of the S^7 Mysteries, it's necessary to give you one more math analogy. (This is the last one, we promise!)

In life, there are choices we make that can have an *additive* effect, and there are choices we make that can have a *multiplier* effect. So things like putting your keys in the same place every time so you can find them or a night of uninterrupted sleep or getting ice cream—these positive choices have an additive effect on your life and make going through your day a little bit better. But there are also things that can have a multiplier effect. Being in love or working out regularly or getting an education—these have a multiplying impact over many facets of your life, with implications far beyond day-by-day living.

Looking at it mathematically, a string of events ("S" being the events) that are additive in nature look like this:

$$S + S + S + S + S + S + S$$

And a string of events ("S" being the events) that are multipliers look like this:

$$S \times S \times S \times S \times S \times S \times S$$

The S^7 Mysteries have a multiplier effect on your spiritual life. To understand the dramatic difference mathematically, let's replace the letter "S" with the number "10":

Additive Effect:
$$10 + 10 + 10 + 10 + 10 + 10 + 10 = 70$$

Seventy is a big number. But let's try multiplying 10 by itself 7 times:

Multiplier Effect:
$$10 \times 10 \times 10 \times 10 \times 10 \times 10 \times 10 = 10,000,000$$

Ten million! We're no statisticians, but ten million is bigger than seventy. And that's the significance of committing to living out these S^7 Mysteries. Every time you make one of these areas a practice in your life, it leads to an exponential increase in your faith.

It's the difference between a faith that shows up to church nineteen times a year and a faith that smiles and forgives in the face of torture and death.

Let's take a look at each of the S⁷ Mysteries and see where you and your church stand.

SURRENDER

If there is a God, you are, in a sense, alone with Him. You cannot put Him off with speculations about your next-door neighbours or memories of what you have read in books. What will all that chatter and hearsay count (will you even be able to remember it?) when the anesthetic fog which we call 'nature' or 'the real world' fades away and the Presence in which you have always stood becomes palpable, immediate, and unavoidable?

—C. S. LEWIS, *MERE CHRISTIANITY*

The earliest Christians were surrendered to God in ways we have never experienced. Keep in mind that in the middle of a hostile culture, their decision to follow Jesus often came with fatal consequences, yet they did it anyway. For the Early Church, death to self wasn't just a metaphor.

We're not suggesting that modern believers need to be on the brink of martyrdom all the time, but it is clarifying, is it not? Their stark choice to surrender to God in the face of persecution is particularly jarring when compared to many of today's churches that have designed their entire program around avoiding any sort of distress for their parishioners. "We don't want to make people uncomfortable" is the silent slogan at many houses of worship. A few years ago, we visited a church that discouraged people from bringing their Bibles to the services. They felt that having a Bible might be intimidating or uncomfortable to a new visitor sitting next to you.

Even the centuries-old concept of surrendering your life to Jesus has been business-class comforted up to "accepting Jesus." Just consider that word choice for a second: we've taken what was for the Early Church a hauntingly holy moment of total capitulation akin to signing your own death warrant . . . and turned it into a personal decision closer to hemming and hawing whether to sign for a FedEx package or not.

To *surrender* is our heart admitting our weakness. To *accept* is our ego demanding the illusion of still being in charge.

Even if we finally yearn to break away from That Other God, in today's selfie culture that will be far more difficult than we think. But it must start with the recognition that we play no part in the transaction. Jesus says clearly in John 15:16, "You did not choose me, but I chose you."

In his book, *Prodigal God*, Pastor Tim Keller goes even further and forces us to pour Drano on our ego and dissolve it entirely. He takes aim not at our willingness to repent of our *obvious* sins, but at our unwillingness to wrestle with the prideful delusion of our perceived morality:

> To truly become a Christian we must also repent of the reasons we ever did anything right. Pharisees only

repent of their sins, but Christians repent for the very roots of their righteousness, too. We must learn to repent of the sin under all our other sins and under all our righteousness—the sin of seeking to be our own Savior and Lord. We must admit that we've put our ultimate hope and trust in things other than God, and that in both our wrongdoing and right doing we have been seeking to get around God or get control of God in order to get hold of those things.

Moses didn't have a say in the bush burning near him. Mary didn't get to choose if the angel suddenly appeared. Paul had absolutely no control on the Damascus Road. That Other God lets us pretend to play a role in accepting Jesus, but God demands that our surrender be unconditional.

Surrender is the key that unlocks the other six mysteries. Without it, we remain stuck at square one.

SCRIPTURE

A Bible that's falling apart usually belongs to someone who isn't.

—AUTHOR AND PASTOR CHARLES HADDON SPURGEON

Early in this book, we laid out the scandalous statistics of how rarely even regular church attenders read the Bible. No need in this chapter to measure our waistlines again; we know we're fat.

But while the lack of frequency is in the data, what's not evident in those numbers is wavelength. Put another way, is your daily Bible engagement pretty much the length of time it takes to read a devotional while on the toilet?

> All Scripture is inspired by God and is useful to teach us what is true and to make us realize what is wrong in our lives. It corrects us when we are wrong and teaches us to do what is right. God uses it to prepare and equip his people to do every good work. (2 Timothy 3:16–17 NLT)

Laid before us is a Book. Breathed into it are the divine secrets of the universe. Woven into every page is our Creator's revealed plan for our daily lives and our eternal destiny. Yet we think so little of the Bible that even committed believers read it only when it's convenient. That Other God doesn't mind, though. That Other God knows how busy we are with, you know, other stuff.

By contrast, the church fathers (men like Ignatius, Polycarp, Clement, and Barnabas) vigorously spent time in the Scriptures. Their relentless pursuit of God's Word gave them the tools they needed to courageously defend Christianity against heresies that were coming from all directions. And in their work, *their single source of authority was Scripture.*

Listen to what these Early Church leaders said about engagement with the Scriptures:

Origen (AD 185–254): The Word of God is in your heart. The Word digs in this soil so that the spring may gush out.

Jerome (AD 342–420): You are reading? No. Your betrothed is talking to you! It is your betrothed, that is, Christ, who is united with you. He tears you away from the solitude of the desert and brings you into his home, saying to you, "Enter into the joy of your Master."

John Chrysostom (AD 347–407): Listen carefully to me: procure books [of the Bible] that will be medicines for the soul. At least get a copy of the New Testament, the apostle's Epistles, the Acts, the Gospels, for your constant teachers. If you encounter grief, dive into them as into a chest of medicines; take from them comfort for your trouble, whether it be loss, or death, or bereavement over the loss of relations. Don't simply dive into them. Swim in them. Keep them constantly in your mind. The cause of all evils is the failure to know the Scriptures well.

"But when?" the modern believer asks. "Where would I find the time?"

The answer can be found in Joshua 1:8: "The Book of the Law shall not depart from your mouth, but you shall meditate on it day and night." The verse concludes with a fascinating—and paradoxical—cause and effect: "For then you will make your way prosperous, and then you will have good success." A hearty meal of Scripture in the morning and evening isn't time consuming but instead helps focus our day and is beneficial to our daily needs. How is that possible?

We must let go of the fallacy that human logic is the only

answer to every question. When we daily infuse ourselves in the Bible, there is a new force at work in our lives. Be assured that if you put the God who created the sun, moon, and stars first in your life, then He can surely reorient your day more efficiently. As Dallas Willard wrote in *The Divine Conspiracy,* "The heavens progressively open to us as our character and understanding are increasingly attuned to the realities of God's rule from the heavens."

If surrender is the key to the lock, then consistent Scripture reading is the mystery that pushes open the ancient rusted gate.

SUBMISSION

Ability to resist temptation is directly proportionate to your submission to God.

—MEN'S MINISTRY LEADER ED COLE

Perhaps no other word of the S⁷ Mysteries offends the modern ear more than the idea of submission. It seems like one of those long-abandoned notions—like indentured servitude or leeching—that was left in the dustbin of history for good reason.

Submission offends us because it presents a direct challenge to our philosophy of self-importance. For most of us, That Other God did away with such primitive requirements long ago in favor of a more mutually respectful, egalitarian relationship.

**Yet if you've yielded to surrender and finally seen
the importance of Scripture in your life,
then submission is the next critical step.**

Submission to God is a key principle in the Bible, and it is made most evident in two areas: community compliance to church authority, and personal obedience to Scripture.

In the case of church authority, the New Testament notes the offices, requirements, and responsibilities of pastors, deacons, elders, and bishops, because for the Early Church, submission by the community mattered. The movement was in its beginning stages, and unity among believers was desperately needed.

Today, that sense of unity is all but lost. In cities across America, Christians change attendance and membership with such frequency that the term "church hopper" is now in our lexicon. Sadly, we know of a church that lost hundreds of members on a single Sunday when the cool, new church opened up a few blocks away. The internet has also given rise to Christians who "feel called" to criticize their local church through blogs and social media, instead of working through disagreements in person as the Bible outlines.

The greatest tragedy of our loss of submission to church authority is pastors who fall into sin through sexual, financial, or other wrongdoing. We're often called for advice by local churches in the wake of those scandals to help them respond to the congregation, to the community, and to the press. As a result, we can confirm the heartbreaking number of cases where fallen pastors refuse to submit to other leaders for healing and restoration. Often, they simply move to another part of town and start a new church or, incredibly, stay where they are and never miss a day on the pulpit. In the case of the latter, we're not sure which is worse—pastors living in sin whose pride keeps them on the pulpit, or their church members who don't care.

Vast numbers of Christians have moved so far away from obedience to Scripture that they pick and choose doctrine to suit their own whims. This plague is so ubiquitous now in American Christianity that "cafeteria Christian" could describe a significant part of our community.

But what if we decided to honor God by submitting ourselves to church authority and obedience to Scripture? What if we looked at our local church not through the lens of "how does it serve me," but rather "how can I serve it"? What if we leaned into the Bible verses that challenge and offend us and, through prayer, asked God to help us understand and obey them?

Impossible, you say?

If we did, we'd be modeling ourselves after the Master. In an extraordinary passage in the letter to the church in Philippi, Paul explained Christ's obedience and the humble submission required of us as well:

> Have this mind among yourselves, which is yours in Christ Jesus, who, though he was in the form of God, did not count equality with God a thing to be grasped, but emptied himself, by taking the form of a servant, being born in the likeness of men. And being found in human form, he humbled himself by becoming

obedient to the point of death, even death on a cross. (Philippians 2:5–8)

Jesus understood what we have forgotten: that we need submission in our lives to achieve God's desire to restore humanity—and He calls us to follow His example. But ironically, total submission actually leads to *more* liberty, not less. John Newton, the reformed slaver and lyricist of "Amazing Grace," once penned the following verse. It explains the mystery of submission at work in real time:

To see the Law by Christ fulfilled,
And hear His pardoning voice,
Transforms the slave into a child,
And duty into choice.

Could it be that the shackles of addiction and sin are actually *loosened* by submission?

There's only one way to know for sure.

SERVICE

For you were called to freedom, brothers. Only do not use your freedom as an opportunity for the flesh, but through love serve one another.

—GALATIANS 5:13

It's not like Christians don't know that we are biblically obliged to participate in acts of service. We know! But let's be brutally candid with each other—serving others is messy. It takes a lot of time. Sometimes these people smell. The worst are the ones who don't even show gratitude for what we did for them. Plus, there are experts who do Christian service for a living, and they can do *a much better job* than we ever could. It's much easier to farm out the work of service to a professional charity or ministry organization than to get our hands dirty.

All of that is 100 percent true. And that's why That Other God always recommends we just write a check to mollify any pangs of guilt we might be feeling. Plus, there's the bonus of a tax deduction—don't forget to get a receipt!

But the further we inch away from That Other God, the louder we hear Jesus's call and personal example to serve others. Henri Nouwen, in *The Selfless Way of Christ*, puts it this way:

> It's not enough to try and imitate Christ as much as possible; it is not enough to be inspired by the words and actions of Jesus Christ. No, the spiritual life presents us with a far more radical demand: to be living Christs here and now, in time and history. We will never know our true vocation in life unless we are willing to grapple with the radical claim the gospel places on us. . . . Regardless of the particular shape we give to our lives, Jesus's call to discipleship is primal, all-encompassing, all-inclusive, demanding a total commitment. One

cannot be a little bit for Christ, give him some attention or make him one of many concerns.

This has explosive implications. When Jesus says in Matthew 20:28 that "the Son of Man came not to be served but to serve," He means that when we help someone, we're actually taking on the character of Christ. Suddenly, "service" isn't what it looks like on the outside at all!

So the teenager helping in the church nursery, the dad coaching in a local youth sports league, the recovering alcoholic providing loving guidance for someone struggling with drugs—they are becoming living examples of Christ through service.

These mysteries work in tandem with one another to impact us in exponential ways. The janitor cleaning the church, the woman bringing lunch and friendship to a shut-in elderly couple, and the usher who anonymously sets up the chairs in the prayer room are becoming more like Jesus with every deed.

And history has proven time and again, service not only helps us but also transforms entire cultures. The early Christians attracted the attention of the Romans by racing to the heart of places hit by the plague when well-to-do Romans were racing in the other direction. Throughout history Christians have built leper colonies, hospitals, and schools in the most challenging places and with people of other religious and cultural beliefs.

Even today in North Korea, a country where people are arrested for owning a Bible, the Ignis Community is a Christian outreach that openly operates under the watchful eye of the

Communist leadership. The reason? They founded a program in Pyongyang to help children with disabilities (particularly cerebral palsy) learn to walk. In addition to working with severely disabled children, the Ignis Community also distributes medicine, food, and other essentials to the remotest areas of the country. Since their service to the disabled community in North Korea is making such a difference, and since there are virtually no other treatment programs for cerebral palsy in the entire country, the government not only allows this ministry to continue but *financially supports the effort.*

Self-centered, self-absorbed Christians are capable of such world-changing actions only when they are willing to surrender, willing to follow the commands of Scripture, willing to submit to authority, and willing to serve others. Then, and only then, do we find ourselves mysteriously transformed into the image of Jesus.

SACRIFICE

He is no fool who gives what he cannot keep to gain what he cannot lose.

—MISSIONARY JIM ELLIOT

Here, the way back to God takes a sharp, steep turn toward our final three mysteries. Be warned: all three disciplines strike fatal blows to our comfortable, consumer-driven, controlling hearts. So it is at this place where That Other God feels most threatened and fights hardest to retain primacy in our lives.

For most of us, the idea of sacrifice is understood and practiced only in terms of dieting. We give up chocolate for Lent, or we may participate in fasting (that's conveniently timed to the upcoming party we are attending and the dress we need to fit into). But for Christians to truly understand sacrifice and its role as a mystery that brings us closer to Jesus, we need to hear about the saints around us who became living sacrifices.

People like Jim and Elisabeth Elliot, young missionaries in Ecuador in 1956. While attempting to reach out to the Auca tribe (also known as Huaorani or Waodani), Jim was martyred by the people he was serving. Rather than fleeing to the United States for safety, Elisabeth and a small group of other missionary wives, whose husbands were also killed in the attack, decided to stay in that country and continue the efforts to reach the very warriors who had killed their husbands. Eventually, Elisabeth and her friends led the tribe to Christ.

Or Dr. Paul Brand, who was born to missionary parents in the mountains of southwestern India in 1914. After medical training in London, he was tempted to choose a lucrative career as an orthopedic surgeon. But instead, he and his wife returned to Vellore, India, to teach at the Christian Medical College and Hospital. As the school's first professor of orthopedics and hand research, Dr. Brand did pioneering work with those suffering from Hansen's disease, a bacterial infection more commonly known as leprosy. Since ancient times, leprosy had been a terrifying disease that caused people to be shunned by and cast out of normal society. Brand was the first surgeon to use reconstructive surgery to correct deformities caused by the disease, and he developed techniques for prevention and healing still being used today. Brand performed more than three thousand surgeries at the Christian

Medical College as a worldwide authority on leprosy, eventually becoming president of the London-based Leprosy Mission International. His insights on the importance and value of pain are described in his book with Philip Yancey, *Pain: The Gift Nobody Wants.*

Most of us hear these inspiring stories but think such commitment and bravery are beyond our capacities. The truth is, modern disciples like Elliot and Brand and ancient believers like Abraham and Abel internalized the same simple truth found in Scripture—that God created everything:

> For by him all things were created, in heaven and on earth, visible and invisible, whether thrones or dominions or rulers or authorities—all things were created through him and for him. (Colossians 1:16)

Why is creation important to sacrifice?

Suppose we are neighbors, and every tool in your garage is mine. I've given you some, and you've borrowed some; but every single tool in there belongs to me—and we both know it. One day I humbly come to your door with a project that needs one of the twenty shovels leaning against the wall in your garage. Aren't you more than willing (almost embarrassingly so) to give me one of my shovels back to complete the job? Perhaps you even recognize my overwhelming generosity over the years and offer to help me.

When we realize that everything we have and everything we are is God's and not ours, then sacrifice doesn't seem like a sacrifice at all. Tithing, volunteering, and mission work stop feeling like a chore and start feeling like us giving back what wasn't ours in the first place. This is what makes it possible for ordinary people to give up extraordinary things—homes, careers, money, reputations, and even people they love the most. For the God who gave us everything, including His Son, sacrifice becomes our gift back to Him.

British missionary explorer David Livingstone said, "If a commission by an earthly king is considered an honor, how can a commission by a heavenly king be considered a sacrifice?"

SIMPLICITY

Simplicity is the only thing that sufficiently reorients our lives so that possessions can be genuinely enjoyed without destroying us.

—RICHARD FOSTER, *CELEBRATION OF DISCIPLINE*

There's no question that our modern world runs at a pace never seen before. With an explosion of mobile devices and other screens demanding our attention, we are bombarded with data. One measurable example: advertising research calculates that every single day we see up to five thousand media messages! With so many opportunities at our fingertips to gain knowledge, wealth, success, why does contentment feel further and further away?

One of the things That Other God constantly whispers in our ear is, "You need that." The average American household now has almost $16,000 in credit card debt. Comedian Will Rogers said it well: "Too many people spend money they haven't earned to buy things they don't want to impress people they don't like."

But Jesus had a better way.

Uh-oh, you may be thinking, *You guys are setting me up. Here comes the totally unrealistic ideal that Jesus wants me to sell all my possessions. That's not going to happen.*

Relax. Not true.

We often assume that the ancient world Jesus lived in has no relevance to our modern world. But Jesus had plenty of rich and upwardly mobile friends just like we do. As we discover in Luke 8, traveling in His close circle of followers were some wealthy women who funded Jesus and His disciples' itinerant ministry. (Somebody had to pay the bill for thirteen guys to go without steady jobs for three years!) But while Jesus often spoke of the dangerous allure of money and possessions, He wasn't calling for their total elimination from our lives. Rather, He was challenging us to pursue something *much* more revolutionary. He was calling us to simplicity.

Simplicity demands that nothing get in the way of our relationship to God.

Here is another counterintuitive, paradoxical mystery. As Jesus's followers, by choosing less in every area of our lives, we gain more. When we allow the Holy Spirit to search our hearts to streamline our desires, we slowly acquire proper perspective—His perspective. With it, our urgent desire to relentlessly consume fades.

As Jesus told the woman at the well in John 4:13–14:

> Everyone who drinks of this water will be thirsty again, but whoever drinks of the water that I will give him will never be thirsty again. The water that I will give him will become in him a spring of water welling up to eternal life.

A second benefit of simplicity is others' perception of us. The book of Acts gives an extraordinary account of the early Christians:

> All who believed were together and had all things in common. And they were selling their possessions and belongings and distributing the proceeds to all, as any had need. And day by day, attending the temple together and breaking bread in their homes, they received their food with glad and generous hearts, praising God and having favor with all the people. And the Lord added to their number day by day those who were being saved. (Acts 2:44–47)

We gain a few key insights in this passage. First, these believers still had homes. While they were selling some possessions and distributing the proceeds, they didn't sell everything. So what were they doing? They were simplifying! Second, simplicity led to unity, generosity, and joy. Finally, simplicity was infectious. Not only did they find "favor with all the people," but their example inspired others to join their ranks.

Imagine in our stressful, consumption-fueled society a community of tens of millions of people who never thirst and seem to possess what money and power can't buy—peace and contentment. What a beacon we would be!

This is the direct result of simplicity, and its benefits are available to anyone and everyone. We just have to get to it.

SUFFERING

It is eternally impossible to preach what Christianity is in truth without having to suffer for it in this world.

—SØREN KIERKEGAARD, *ATTACK UPON "CHRISTENDOM"*

In the Italian town of Bevagna, there is a small church, Sant' Agostino. Built in 1316 just outside the Roman walls of the medieval city, the chapel is tiny compared to most, but it's filled with frescos dating back more than five hundred years. Incredibly, this priceless collection of art was only recently rediscovered. At some point around World War II, the parishioners and caretakers of St. Agostino decided the interior walls of the church should be plastered over and painted white.

In the 1980s, the local priest was doing a small repair job on a wall of the chapel. As he scraped through the plaster to repair a crack, a pair of eyes stared back at him. He immediately called in art restoration experts, and as they carefully removed more plaster, they discovered an ancient fresco—and then another, and another. The restoration continues to this day.

Even more interesting than the discovery of the hidden

artistic treasure is the choice of image on the main fresco—a depiction of early Christians being tortured. One character is having his teeth pulled out. Another just had her breast cut off—horrifying, typical methods of torture and execution throughout history. Apparently in 1316, the builders and patrons of the church wanted to pay great tribute to those who had suffered for their faith. But it seems that by the 1940s, that message may have been too strong for the members of St. Agostino, so they plastered it over and painted it white.

For most of Christianity's history, persecution has been part of life. Even today, persecution is the norm for much of the world's non-Western Christians. Arrest for worshipping at an unlicensed house church is common in China. Dismemberment and torture by Boko Haram is the risk you take for being a Christian in Nigeria. Being driven from your home, losing your job, or even death by beheading is the punishment for being a Christian in many parts of the Islamic world. In *The Insanity of God* about Christian persecution, Russian pastor, Nik Ripkin, said, "For us, persecution is like the sun coming up in the east. It happens all the time. It's the way things are. There is nothing unusual or unexpected about it."

In the West, the idea of suffering for the gospel is virtually unknown. This is because most Western democracies have laws protecting freedom of religion. But that's only part of the story.

It's not a coincidence that in parts of the world where persecution still exists, people there are on fire to share the gospel of Jesus. This is a quality they share with the earliest Christians, who were so aligned with Jesus that they were honored to suffer as He did. Across the pages of the Bible and throughout history, there is a direct correlation between evangelism and persecution. But in most modern Christian circles, evangelism is dead. We've stopped sharing the story of Jesus.

We have gone silent as a trade-off to avoid any sort of discrimination, and it is to our everlasting shame.

Back in the 1940s, English crime writer Dorothy Sayers warned of a fast-approaching church that would be too comfortable and tolerant to make any waves:

> In the world it calls itself tolerance; but in hell it is called despair. . . . It is the sin that believes in nothing, cares for nothing, seeks to know nothing, interferes with nothing, enjoys nothing, loves nothing, hates nothing, finds purpose in nothing, lives for nothing, and remains alive only because there is nothing it would die for.

The Bible is not kinder. In John's vision in the book of Revelation, Jesus says to the church in Laodicea:

> Because you are lukewarm, and neither hot nor cold, I will spit you out of my mouth. For you say, I am rich, I have prospered, and I need nothing, not realizing that you are wretched, pitiable, poor, blind, and naked. (Revelation 3:16–18)

We, too, have plastered over the images of the Christian life we find disagreeable. But the eternal beauty of Christ's call to embrace the risks of evangelism will not be silenced by our man-made, whitewashed walls.

Here the way back encounters a deep and dangerous crevasse—one that can only be overcome when the exponential power of the other S^7 Mysteries are put into practice.

When we . . .

- surrender our futures to the Creator;
- immerse ourselves in Scripture;
- submit to the authority of God, His Word, and His church;
- choose love and service to others;
- seek to sacrifice what we have been given as a gift back to Him; and
- focus our lives in simplicity to be living examples to others;

. . . then we can step out in faith across the crevasse and be prepared for the days of suffering. What happens when we step out is different for every child of God.

To live these S^7 Mysteries—to choose the transformed life and share the message of Jesus— is to embrace the eventuality of suffering.

As we survey the diminishing impact of the church in our lifetime and compare it to the astonishing impact the Early Church had in their culture, this unique mix of behaviors is where the difference lies. The S⁷ Mysteries are the call of Jesus that radically transformed the world two thousand years ago and can do it again today. They are the path back to the miraculous, where the spiritually crippled see our example, believe, then pick up their mat and follow in our steps. These ancient values are the keys that unlock the ability to lovingly confound and convict an uninterested and hostile culture. In the apostle Peter's first letter, he says:

> You are a chosen race, a royal priesthood, a holy nation, a people for his own possession, that you may proclaim the excellencies of him who called you out of darkness into his marvelous light. (1 Peter 2:9)

The King James Version's majestic translation of that verse refers to us as "a peculiar people." What a laudable goal! May we never forget again how truly unique we are.

These S⁷ Mysteries are worth spending serious time considering. As the two of us studied and meditated on each of these spiritual practices, the reality check of what it means to be an authentic Christian began taking hold, and we believe the same could happen to you.

PART THREE

THE PURGE

No one who has ever bowed before the burning bush
can thereafter speak lightly of God.

A. W. TOZER,
CULTURE

WAKE-UP CALLS are wonderfully terrifying things. Like a child turning on the light in a strange room, there is a moment of fear (*Are there monsters in there?*) and then enchantment with the unknown possibilities.

For adults, those wake-up calls are more like the bloated feeling after the holiday season. We've eaten ourselves into a stupor, realize the need to join a local gym, and steel ourselves for the hard work ahead. Most never last beyond the first couple of months of CrossFit classes, but for those who really desire change, everything becomes focused on next steps.

If we have recognized the importance of the S^7 Mysteries, then it's time to act.

The first step is to start clearing things out.

CHAPTER 7

CLEANING OUT THE FRIDGE

The truth does not change according
to our ability to stomach it emotionally.

NOVELIST FLANNERY O'CONNOR

You are called to a mission! Not just to bask
in his glory on the mountaintop, but to share
his message with a lost and dying world.

PASTOR JACK GRAHAM

OVER AND OVER, Christians throughout history who accomplished significant things in the world first experienced a moment when they faced the stark reality of truth. For some, those Damascus Road–type experiences may have been crying out to God in a storm or seeing the transformation of someone else's life. Many young couples attribute that moment to the birth of a child, soldiers have experienced it in battle, and others had the experience while simply reading a passage from the Bible. In that moment, it's as if space and time is torn, and a person is given of glimpse of reality beyond anything they have ever experienced.

They are never the same again.

A moment like this has launched many of the greatest evangelistic, missionary, and social transformations in history. Artists and poets call that moment an epiphany. The Bible calls it a revelation.

Most of us think of "revelation" only as the title of the last book in the Bible. You know—the one you never read because you think it's too hard and, frankly, too weird. (We understand!) But the book of Revelation's vivid imagery is a wake-up call to what lies ahead for humanity. It's time for us to have reality check about how we've been living our lives as believers in an unbelieving world.

Nothing can destroy Christianity if we live like Christians.

—A. W. TOZER, *CULTURE*

A tree that falls in a storm usually isn't felled by the outside force of the wind. It falls because it's already rotten on the inside. The same is true of Christians.

A few years ago, we produced a men's small group video teaching series hosted by two Navy SEALs. We discovered the training that goes into becoming a SEAL is so grueling that the final week is called Hell Week. They describe it as the most extreme test of mental toughness. The trainees must endure nonstop pain, sleep deprivation, and freezing temperatures. The goal is to maximize their performance under the most challenging physical and emotional stresses.

Think about it for a minute—the trainees are soaking wet, bitterly cold, doing full-on physical training for five and a half days—and getting only a few hours of sleep at night. They take in about 7,000 calories a day, but with the intense training involved, they still lose weight. The result? Only about 25 percent of the candidates make it through.

But those 25 percent are incredibly committed, highly skilled, and very motivated warriors.

What if we took Christianity as seriously as Navy SEALs take their training?

We don't recommend Hell Week, but the truth is, Christians are losing the battle for our culture because we would rather skip the training. We'd rather pursue *our* dreams than do the hard work of discovering *God's* dreams.

You won't find many books written about how difficult Christianity can be. After all, it's much easier to get a larger audience by teaching about God's goodness or His grace. Yes, those attributes of God are important. God *is* a good God. But if we never go deeper, then we will never experience what it's like to walk in the presence and power of the living God. More to our point, we'll never make much of an impact on the world.

ARE YOU READY TO START TRAINING?

So, what should we do? When you are trying to get in shape and shed a few pounds, the first stop is the refrigerator. Purging the fridge of ice cream, cookie dough, sodas, and frozen dinners is the first step toward making a significant change. As the saying goes, "The thinking it took to get us into this mess is not the same thinking that is going to get us out of it."

As we start our training, here are a handful of things worth purging from the fridge.

OUR EGOS

Let's start by dumping the idea that "it's all about me." That belief alone will dramatically change our perspective on living the Christian life. Instead of being so "inward" thinking, it's time to get "outward" in our thinking.

Here's a good scale to measure our progress: How many times do we say "I" or "me" in our prayers?

Oh—and here's another one: Do we search for a church because it meets *our* needs? We can't find any directions in the Bible for evaluating a church because we liked the music, we liked the way the pastor preached, or it was easy to park.

Or better yet, do we attend a large church because we can be anonymous and don't have to actually meet anyone?

How many Christian books, sermons, and conferences are about discovering your destiny or finding your purpose in life? But throughout the life of Jesus, we find He was pursuing God's will, not His own.

It's not about us.

And for the record, speaking of losing our ego, we can't do the Christian life alone. As Brian Houston, global senior pastor of Hillsong Church, puts it in *How to Maximise Your Life,* "Don't be fooled into thinking that you have the capacity to achieve your best on your own. A training partner in the gym is a great asset because when you think you have reached your limit, there is someone who can push you to go further."

OUR DEFENSIVENESS

Pastor Drew Sams of Bel Air Church tells the story of a college roommate who had the nerve to look Drew in the eye and tell him Drew wasn't a Christian. For most of us who consider ourselves believers, that would be pretty offensive. How dare he? But the roommate had enough moral courage and loving concern for his friend to tell him that by comparing what the Bible teaches with the standards of Drew's behavior, Drew couldn't possibly be a Christian.

Most people might have complained to the dean, or at the very least changed roommates. But that moment of revelation—*a reality check*—stopped Drew in his tracks and made him realize his roommate was exactly right. That moment of truth, expressed in love and respect, completely changed the direction of Drew's life. Rather than becoming defensive, offended, or angry, Drew took it to heart, took the right action, and is now the pastor of a remarkable church in the heart of Los Angeles.

I've always said that I don't respect people who don't proselytize. I don't respect that at all. If you believe that there's a heaven and a hell, and people could be going to hell or not getting eternal life, and you think that it's not really worth telling them this because it would make it socially awkward . . . how much do you have to hate somebody to not proselytize? How much do you have to hate somebody to believe everlasting life is possible and not tell them that?

—MAGICIAN AND ENTERTAINER (AND ATHEIST)

PENN JILLETTE

OUR PRIDEFULNESS

Be quick to apologize to critics who are 100 percent right. Ouch. We're hitting close to home. But these critics are the men and women who walked away from God because of what they saw in the lives of believers, such as hypocrisy, abuse, anger, inattention, lying—we could go on and on. In these cases, there is no easy response because it's completely understandable that after seeing how some Christians act, these men and women would turn away.

We can find examples of this everywhere. The most public Christian platforms are often filled with the most embarrassing misrepresentations of what it is to be like Christ. While many great media outreaches are doing remarkable things to share the gospel, too many others are driving people away. For instance, Christian media—which is often the most visible presence for the gospel to nonbelievers—still features radio stations, TV stations, and networks that broadcast programs that are error-filled or wacky at best, and outright heretical at worst.

Why does this matter? In our experience, when you share Christ with a nonbeliever, they often throw back in your face a bad televangelist—someone who drives a Rolls-Royce, whose ministry is all about money, or who has had a long string of divorces. We've seen people reject God after watching a beloved pastor cheat on his wife, a Christian boss embezzle money from the company, or a Christian friend turn on them.

When a Christian doesn't live as a Christian should, the damage is done.

But there's hope. In the marketing world, we have a term called *low-hanging fruit*. It means those who would be most likely to buy a product or who once owned the product are the easiest to reach with the advertising message. While we obviously want to reach everyone with the gospel, in the church today we spend the vast majority of our time worrying about the hard cases, while there are millions of others who are *so close* to accepting the message of Jesus. Those millions are the men and women who have turned away from God because Christians haven't lived out our calling. They could be considered low-hanging fruit. They once believed, or at the very least were open to the message of the gospel.

Certainly, there are nonbelievers out there who have a grudge against God, are convinced He doesn't exist, or enjoy living in sin. But think about it: without any overt evangelism, just living our lives as committed believers, we could change the minds of those millions of men and women who once were open but turned away.

HAVE WE BECOME
TOO CASUAL ABOUT GOD?

In our well-intentioned effort to make worship more casual and encourage people to "come as you are," we have developed worship leaders who appear to be singing to their boyfriend and pastors who pray in public as if talking to a buddy from middle school.

As a result, it's easy to look at the biblical virtue of holiness as unattractive, or a lifestyle meant only for desert monks or the Mother Teresa–types of the world. But the truth is, holy living is far more fascinating to the nonbelieving culture than we think. True holiness isn't about being uptight or a stick-in-the-mud; it's about recognizing the majesty and holy presence of God and then reflecting that to the world.

In his commentary on the gospel of Mark, theologian R. C. Sproul writes:

At the beginning of the twentieth century, a German theologian and sociologist studied human beings' reactions to whatever they deemed to be holy, and he found that holiness is both terrifying and fascinating to the sinner. We know that we are not holy. We know that our lives are not right. However, we do not want to hear judgments against us. Therefore, we fear that which is holy. That is why Mark tells us that Herod "feared John." His fear was not the result of any power John had to harm Herod. Rather, it was because he knew John was "a just and holy man." And yet, when the holy comes near, as fearful as it is, we have a certain attraction to it. Thus, even in his fear, Herod wanted to hear John talk. He was both fearful of John and drawn to him.

Nothing is fresher in the modern world than real orthodoxy.

—AUTHOR ROD DREHER

A lifestyle of holiness gets noticed from a world in moral free fall. When a nonbeliever comes in contact with a life of holiness, they notice. If R. C. Sproul is right, living a life of holiness is far more effective than judgment or criticism when it comes to transforming the culture, because encountering a life of holiness creates conviction that begins a search for answers.

THE WORLD IS WATCHING

We must never forget that the world is watching how we treat each other—and what they see can be far more powerful than what we teach. As it is, it's no surprise that Christians do a less-than-stellar job when it comes to our attitudes toward each other and the world. It's that kind of criticism that prompted Gandhi's famous quote: "I like your Christ. I do not like your Christians. Your Christians are so unlike your Christ."

And his follow-up: "If it weren't for Christians, I'd be a Christian."

Once we've purged the fridge, we can start thinking about the challenge we face.

CHAPTER 8

STOP THINKING EVERYONE HATES US

We can no longer excuse these failures by arguing
that the surrounding culture is secular
and hostile to spiritual matters,
for that is manifestly not the case.

JOHN DRANE,
CULTURAL CHANGE AND BIBLICAL FAITH

To clasp the hands in prayer is the beginning
of an uprising against the disorder of the world.

THEOLOGIAN KARL BARTH

ASK MOST CHRISTIAN LEADERS TODAY, and they'll describe the culture we live in as pretty hostile to the faith—particularly when it comes to major political and policy issues. There's no question that the news media projects that attitude, but before we can effectively share the gospel story with a neighbor, it's important to know who that neighbor is and what he or she thinks.

A recent Pew Research Center survey found: "All told, about two-thirds of U.S. adults (65 percent) describe themselves as religious (either in addition to be being spiritual or not). Nearly one-in-five say they are spiritual but not religious (18 percent), and about one-in-six say they are neither religious nor spiritual (15 percent)."

But today, there seems to be an overwhelming rise in Christian articles, op-ed pieces, and sermons claiming that the world hates the gospel and discussing what we should do as a result. Typical Christian news sites are filled with stories of Hollywood, the gay community, liberals, feminists, atheists, progressives, and any number of other groups who appear to fight against biblical values and how we should brace ourselves for the conflict. Many Christian responses are a mistaken attempt to fight fire with fire, but even those less prone to battle language still think in terms of an anger strategy.

There are scriptural references that seem to back up that approach. In John 15:18, Jesus said, "If the world hates you, know that it has hated me before it hated you." In 2 Timothy

3:12, Paul promised that all who live godly lives will suffer persecution. The apostles certainly suffered during their ministries. Stephen was stoned to death (Acts 7:53–8:1); Paul was put to death by a Roman emperor (2 Timothy 4:6–8); James was beheaded (Acts 12:1–3); John was exiled to the island of Patmos (Revelation 1:9). There's plenty of biblical evidence that for most leaders in the Early Church, their message of this new Savior wasn't very welcome.

Or was it?

When you look a bit closer, some interesting things turn up. For instance, the gospel of Mark is filled with passages of how much the people loved the message of Jesus. In the first four chapters alone there are at least eleven references to the large crowds who came to hear His message. For instance:

- "*All* the country of Judea and *all* Jerusalem were going out to him" (Mark 1:5).
- "And at once his fame spread *everywhere*" (Mark 1:28).
- "And the *whole city* was gathered together at the door" (Mark 1:33).
- "And *many* were gathered together, so that there was no more room" (Mark 2:2).

Mark says that Jesus couldn't even openly enter a town because of the crowds. Instead, He went to desolate places, yet they still came to him "from every quarter" (1:45). In Mark 2, we see that Jesus went all the way to the sea, and people still came to Him (2:13). In Mark 3, a *great* crowd followed Him

(3:7). In Mark 4, there was a *very large* crowd (4:1). In Mark 5, a *great* crowd "thronged" about Him (5:24). In Mark 6, so many were coming and going that Jesus and His disciples couldn't even eat (6:31).

While you could argue that these references may be hyperbole, there's no question that multitudes came to hear this new teaching. Mark goes on and on, and the other gospel writers report similar stories. So, who was doing all the hating?

The people loved Jesus, but those in power did not.

One of the most compelling aspects of the gospel message is that it undermines those in power. Jesus preached a message about a *new* kingdom—a kingdom not of this world. It was a message that challenged everything the religious leaders and Romans knew about the dynamics of power. That kind of challenge quite simply wasn't a message anyone with worldly power wanted to hear.

From the moment of Jesus's birth, Herod questioned the wise men who had come to honor this new King. He was suspicious that someone might challenge his throne and dispatched soldiers to seek out this newborn Child. When he realized he'd been tricked by the wise men, Herod became furious, and he "sent and killed all the male children in Bethlehem and in all that region who were two years old or under, according to the time that he had ascertained from the wise men" (Matthew 2:16).

The news of the arrival of Jesus as a baby spooked Herod to the point that he was willing to kill every male child in the entire city in order to protect his own reign.

The shepherds welcomed the Child. Wise men from other countries welcomed the Child. But the most powerful man in that part of the world was shaken to the core.

**It wasn't just a question of *power*.
It was a question of *authority*.**

From the moment Jesus began His teaching ministry, proclaiming the good news of the kingdom, people recognized that this Man taught with *authority*. For local people living under the brutality of Roman rule, that was like water to a man dying of thirst. It gave them hope. It transformed the way they looked at this world and the next.

But to those in power (who *thought* they had authority), it was a frightening message that could change everything. And that message had to be stopped.

The message of the gospel is hated by those whose authority and power it challenges.

That's why we make a mistake today when we assume the greater culture hates the message of the gospel. Certainly, there are ordinary people who aren't interested in becoming a Christian and some who even despise it. But as Elisha said to his servant in 2 Kings 6:16, "Do not be afraid, for those who are with us are more than those who are with them."

People whom we call "cultural elites"—those in mainstream media, political leaders, special interests, activists, or many in academia—often push back against the message of Jesus, and they get most of the publicity. We hear them interviewed on the evening news, see Christians ridiculed on prime-time TV, and see protests by activists. Our children report back from secular universities where atheist professors make fun of Christian beliefs.

As a result, it's easy to understand that since those cultural elites are often the loudest voices in the room, we assume that kind of non-Christian thinking reflects society as a whole. But there is no evidence that those voices reflect the average person. So while the cultural elites fight against the message of the gospel, we believe that the masses are remarkably open to it.

We can personally attest to that fact, having worked in Hollywood for decades. While most Christians would point to Hollywood as ground zero for people hating Christianity, many of us working in the entertainment industry will confirm that, while there are plenty in the business who aren't Christians or interested in becoming one, they are remarkably open to prayer. In fact, Karen Covell, founder of the Hollywood Prayer Network, has had numerous meetings with nonbelieving studio executives, producers, and celebrities over many years. After these meetings she'll ask if she can pray for them. Almost without exception, they enthusiastically say, "Yes!"

On the first day of filming a TV project we produced, a young production assistant asked if anyone on the crew would be open to saying a short prayer before shooting began. While it was a nonbelieving crew working on a secular television show, even the most hard-core, burly film crew members pushed their way to the front to take someone's hand and join in the prayer.

And it may surprise you to know that right now there are Christian prayer and Bible study groups thriving on the campuses of major studios and TV networks in Los Angeles.

> Some wish to live within
> the sound of a Church or Chapel bell;
> I want to run a Rescue Shop
> within a yard of hell.
>
> —BRITISH MISSIONARY C. T. STUDD

Chances are, what's true in Hollywood is true for most industries in America. While the most vocal leaders may be fighting against Christian principles, the fact is, significant numbers in those organizations are open to the power of belief and simply waiting to hear some good news.

For Christianity to make a difference in the culture, we need to purge ourselves of the idea that everyone hates us. They don't. For too long, we've used that excuse as a crutch. As a community, we have to stop fighting battles that don't exist.

CHAPTER 9

STOP PRETENDING
WE'RE IN CHARGE

As I read the birth stories about Jesus I cannot help
but conclude that though the world may be
tilted toward the rich and powerful,
God is tilted toward the underdog.

PHILIP YANCEY,
THE JESUS I NEVER KNEW

THE MEMBERS of the Early Church were underdogs, to say the very least. Living in the margins (and sometimes hiding underground), they had no money, power, or political influence in the greater culture. Getting the message out there would be difficult, and standing fast against those who would silence their message would cost them their lives.

So they had to think differently—*like underdogs.*

As America's Christians purge ourselves of those attitudes that are either false or no longer relevant, one major area needing a good cleanout is our addiction to power. For example, we fancy ourselves "a Christian nation" when studies show only about 20 percent of people show up to church with weekly regularity. About 20 percent of Americans jog regularly—would we say we are a jogging nation?

Authentic Christians are a distinct minority in America. As such, we need to start thinking in an entirely different way. Like the early Christians, it's time we embrace being underdogs!

UNDERDOGS DON'T ASSUME ANYONE IS LISTENING

Underdogs understand reality. They know that in occupied territory the right to be heard must be earned. As the parable of the wedding feast says in Luke 14, if we keep assuming our seat is at the head table, eventually someone more important will arrive and we'll be asked to move to a seat at the bottom of the social register. In fact, much of the reason we aren't listened to much these days is that *we lead with an attitude of entitlement.*

Immediately after the tragedy of 9/11, a major news network hosted a discussion about the US invasion of Afghanistan. The participants included a teacher in the New Age movement, a liberal ecumenical pastor from a mainline denomination, and a conservative radio Bible teacher and pastor. As the debate progressed, everything the Bible teacher said made perfect sense. His biblically based arguments shattered the positions of the New Age teacher and mainline pastor. From a *truth* perspective, the Bible teacher was easily the superior thinker.

But he lost the debate.

Watching on TV, we could see the New Age teacher and mainline pastor were both engaging and interesting. They smiled and made their points (however wrong) humbly and with grace. The Bible teacher, however, couldn't have been more reactionary. We never saw him smile—in fact, he often scowled. He never looked the host in the eye or acknowledged any value in the other participants' arguments. While they were positive and engaging, he was negative and condescending. As a result, to the millions of people watching that program on television, he may have had the best argument, but he lost the debate.

We were so upset that we wrote that Bible teacher a letter and shared our perception. We suggested that if he would just consider changing his *attitude*, it would make a significant difference in how his message was received by the vast national TV audience.

His response?

The Bible teacher didn't care. He told us that his calling was to speak the truth, and he didn't care if people liked him or not when he did it. Now that might seem noble to some readers of this book, and it's certainly a popular position for a number of Christians. They often use this scripture to support that attitude:

For the word of the cross is folly to those who are perishing, but to us who are being saved it is the power of God. (1 Corinthians 1:18)

Some Christians read that verse and assume they'll automatically make enemies. They think, *If "the word of the cross is folly to those who are perishing," then maybe we'll be hated. So get ugly! Stand your ground! It's not our job to be liked; it's our job to speak the truth and let the chips fall where they may. We're not here to make friends!*

The problem with that thinking is that it's not our job to decide who in the culture thinks the gospel is foolish and who thinks it is the bread of life.

If the *message* of the gospel drives people away, so be it. But if our *attitude, behavior, or approach* drives them away, then it's simply wrong.

It's always our responsibility to proclaim the gospel, but we should never assume that it's our right to be listened to by the culture. When they don't listen, we should simply thank them for the opportunity to speak and move on. The apostle Paul boldly shared the gospel wherever he could. But he was never arrogant or a jerk.

A soft answer turns away wrath. (Proverbs 15:1)

Underdogs understand they must be clever to be heard. For example, then president-elect Abraham Lincoln chose Edward Stanton to be his secretary of war, even though Stanton was a strong adversary of Lincoln's. He had told others that Lincoln was "a low cunning clown" and "the original gorilla." Even after his appointment, Stanton didn't let up on his boss. He called Lincoln a fool, but Lincoln never responded in the same way. Laughing at his own imperfections was the method Lincoln used to blunt the sting from Stanton's constant verbal abuse.

Lincoln gained far more by a gracious response than by fighting back. Eventually, when Lincoln died, Stanton called him "the greatest ruler of men the world has ever seen."

UNDERDOGS HAVE THICK SKIN

For underdogs, the battle is far too great to let small offenses stand in our way. Yet many Christian campaigns are driven by strategies based on being offended. When we feel that a corporation, activist organization, or politician has slighted the Christian faith, somebody invariably gets upset and launches an angry petition drive. And trust us—there are some very angry Christians out there! For instance, on Phil's blog at phil-cooke.com, *Christians* have called him:

- A false prophet
- A joke
- Pathetic
- A fraud
- A "special breed of stupid"
- A moron
- Sickening
- A secular humanist
- A coward
- A shill
- Part of "satanic Hollywood"
- Someone who works hard for the devil
- A heretic
- A sellout

We could go on, but you get the idea. A few pitied Phil's "lost soul," and one person emailed him and told him to "enjoy your thirty pieces of silver"—all because Phil put forth a position that person disagreed with.

If Christians are going to fight the significant battles with today's culture, then we need to understand our priorities. Yes, small things can often grow into much bigger threats, and we should always be alert. But when we take such great offense at everyday points of disagreement, we waste our opportunity for a more effective witness.

The apostle Paul was jailed, beaten, and humiliated, yet he was content (Philippians 4:11). Jesus saved His anger for the religious leaders instead of aiming it toward the people who so desperately needed a shepherd.

UNDERDOGS UNDERSTAND
INCREMENTAL SUCCESS

While some of this book is about Christians joining together to make a significant difference in the culture, never forget the critical principle that small things often make a big difference.

One morning when his daughters were in high school, Phil noticed that a city bus stop right outside the school entrance was plastered with advertisements for a racy new television series, in which the lead character was a glamorous prostitute. It was totally inappropriate, since many schoolchildren used that bus stop, so Phil decided to do something about it. But he didn't get upset, stage a protest, write a letter to the editor, or criticize the bus company. He simply called the advertising company, told them the situation, and asked them to exchange the poster with more appropriate advertising. The employee who answered the phone agreed, and within two hours, the ads were gone.

No major protest or petition drive needed. Just a simple phone call.

Sometimes we don't need a fundraising campaign, press release, policy change, new law, or media coverage. Sometimes all we need is to use our noggins, offer a kind word, and reach out.

What talents and skills are hidden in your church?

A few years ago, pastor Ken Foreman at Cathedral of Faith Church in San Jose, California, discovered something surprising about the people who were sitting in his Sunday service.

It all began with a simple idea. Cathedral of Faith decided to poll their congregation. They asked what talents and skills their parishioners had, and how they thought that information could help the church impact their community more effectively. (We wonder how many pastors have ever asked that question.)

One of the results was a shock. In their pews sat a surprisingly large number of dentists. Dentists? Who would have thought? So Ken invited those professionals to meet and asked them another question: "What could you do as dentists to make an impact for Christ in our community?"

They put their heads together and created a free dental clinic. What started as a small clinic has grown into the largest of its kind in the San Francisco Bay area. Its success and impact has been reported on by the largest media outlets in Northern California and featured on national television—and it all began with a simple inquiry from a pastor.

Underdogs know they don't have all the money, resources, or leverage they need to accomplish their goals. So they have to get creative and start small. Perhaps more important, an underdog attitude teaches us that *every Christian should be prepared to make that difference.* Pastor Kevin Harney puts it this way: "If someone came up to a believer and said, 'Hey, I know you're a Christian, and I want to become a Christian—can you help me?' their answer shouldn't be 'Let me call my pastor.'"

UNDERDOGS NEED ALLIES

Underdogs spend less time attacking each other and more time building bridges. They know that relationships matter; and the more unified the movement, the quicker the culture notices. Certainly, there are significant theological differences among some groups, but if we can't join together in our witness for Jesus under the essential doctrines of the church, then we'll simply splinter and slide into oblivion.

In an age when there is so much need in our culture, do we really want to bicker about whether the King James Version is the only legitimate translation of the Bible? Will we continue to go our separate ways because we can't agree on the kind of worship music to use? Is it right to condemn pastors or other leaders because they share their message through television or in movie theaters?

Recently in Los Angeles, a large church was choosing a new pastor. The best candidate was about thirty-three years old. Some of the members weren't happy with the possibility of such a young pastor, so they considered leaving. But an elder gently reminded them that the very Scriptures the church is based on were proclaimed two thousand years ago by another Teacher who started His ministry around the age of thirty.

It's time to stop looking for our differences and start finding the core teachings on which we agree. And in those cases when we don't agree, even the apostle Paul found a reason to rejoice. As he wrote in Philippians 1:15–18:

> Some indeed preach Christ from envy and rivalry, but others from good will. The latter do it out of love, knowing that I am put here for the defense of the gospel. The former proclaim Christ out of selfish ambition, not sincerely but thinking to afflict me in my

imprisonment. What then? Only that in every way, whether in pretense or in truth, Christ is proclaimed, and in that I rejoice.

The Christian, on the contrary, even if he does not make a great show politically, or a great demonstration of revolutionary power, but if he really lives by the power of Christ—if, by hope, he makes the coming of the Kingdom actual—is a true revolutionary.

—JACQUES ELLUL, *THE PRESENCE OF THE KINGDOM*

The Early Church believed God, but they also were scrappy underdogs.

What if we could shift the perception of today's culture to the point that people would at least *consider* the reality of Jesus? What if we could tip the scales from negative to positive? What if the Christian community became so engaging and compelling that people wanted to see what motivated us?

We believe—like the Early Church experienced—that it could change everything.

PART FOUR

THE MAKEOVER

We should not ask, "What is wrong with the world?"
for that diagnosis has already been given.
Rather, we should ask,
"What has happened to the salt and light?"

THEOLOGIAN AND PREACHER JOHN STOTT

IT'S BEEN SAID that America loves comeback stories. It's in our DNA to root for the underdog, since this country started on a one-in-a-million shot. We like the scrappy sort who gets knocked down but, against all odds, gets back up off the mat and wins.

If you flip through cable TV, these sorts of shows permeate our channels. House flipping, weight loss shows, makeover transformations: they're all the same root story.

This is good news for the Christian community, as we are in dire need of a comeback.

Here's the hard truth: even if all of us committed today to walk away from That Other God, even if every Christian in America pursued all seven of the S^7 Mysteries—we've still damaged our brand. And once you have lost people's trust, it's hard to win it back.

So the same old, same old won't work. The non-Christian world isn't going to respond much if we open another hospital. They're not going to be astonished by us cleaning up some trash along the side of a road. And yet another soup kitchen won't change anyone's made-up mind. No, we need something new!

We don't have all the answers, but the goal of this final section is to get us Christians to start thinking new again. We have a few ideas of some cool things we could try. And, hopefully, the following pages will inspire new thoughts from you.

Soup kitchens, free clinics, orphanages, universities, hospitals, after-school programs, toy drives—at some point, all of them were new ideas. If we are going to find our way back, then let's set our minds to astonishing the world again.

After all, America loves comeback stories.

CHAPTER 10

A CRAIGSLIST CHRISTMAS

If we preach the gospel but don't live in a way
that reflects it, our neighbors won't believe it.

GREG FORSTER,
JOY FOR THE WORLD

Never worry about numbers. Help one person at a time
and always start with the person nearest you.

MOTHER TERESA

TO BE HONEST, no one can remember where the idea or the motivation originated. It probably doesn't matter. What does matter are the results.

Several years ago, Jon and his wife, Kelly, felt moved to post a local online ad in the "Free Stuff" section of Craigslist, asking anyone with a serious financial need at Christmas to simply respond. Most readers probably assumed it was a scam, but sure enough, a few moms who were desperate enough responded. For those who responded, the need was never for themselves— instead, they were suffering from every parent's worst nightmare: that they wouldn't be able to afford Christmas gifts for their kids.

So a few days before Christmas, Jon and Kelly arranged to meet them at a local Target. It was a public place, a store they knew, and easy to find. Still, it was Craigslist, and predators are everywhere. But despite the real risks, the moms showed up.

Jon and Kelly enthusiastically met them with shopping carts, introduced themselves, and started asking what their kids would really like for Christmas. After an hour or two the shopping carts were full of toys, clothing, and plenty of food for a once-in-a-lifetime Christmas dinner. A quick trip through the checkout line, and their parental nightmare was transformed into the greatest Christmas of their entire lives.

Grand total at checkout per family? Three hundred and fifty dollars.

Although the event wasn't focused on trying to convert

anyone, Jon and Kelly did share with each woman that it was their faith in God that motivated them to help, and they offered to pray with each mom before she left the store. With tears in their eyes, these mothers could barely express the difference this one kind act of generosity had made in their lives.

The next year, Jon and Kelly went public. They enlisted Phil, his wife, Kathleen, and a group of other friends to join the fun. Once again, they placed the ad, and another group of families responded. With additional people to help buy gifts, they could accept more families in need.

Year after year, the group has grown. Phil and Kathleen enlisted the help of their daughter and son-in-law, who jumped in with great enthusiasm. Jon and Kelly's young daughters are old enough to help, too, by assisting stunned parents (who can't believe this is actually happening to them) to figure out what toys to get for their kids.

Over the years, we've collectively helped hundreds of families make a U-turn on their Christmas nightmare. And we'll let you in on a little secret. These families think we're the ones blessing them. But in truth, they're the ones blessing us! Here are a couple of notes we've received over the years:

When I was going through a really rough time, you were a true angel from above who helped bring joy and happiness to my children on Christmas Day. Thank you for all your help, and I want you to know that since then, things have gotten much better. Please know your generosity will forever be remembered.
—"Julie"

I simply can't express my gratitude. I've told everyone in my family about this, and the response was the same from each of them . . . they simply didn't believe me!! I had to literally show them the emails. You have made such a huge positive impact in our lives. I had made a choice to give it to God this Christmas and he sent me you. You're an angel! Thank you is simply not enough for what you have chosen to do to help. I've attached a picture of all the gifts wrapped and ready to go under our tree! I can't wait to see my five-year-old's reaction when she wakes up! Please keep us in your prayers.
—Ashley Herrera

Because we live in Los Angeles, our team of Santa's Helpers has included film producers, a casting director, actors, and several movie studio and television executives. Most of our team is comprised of entertainment professionals, some of whom wrestle daily with movie budgets close to $200 million. They live incredibly pressured lives and can easily forget the spirit of Christmas due to project deadlines, studio demands, and business. But the minute they arrive at the store, all that pressure is left behind. For one night, they can focus on a family in need and their ability to make this Christmas special for someone else.

WILL OUR SMALL GROUP OF FRIENDS CHANGE THE WORLD?

Realistically, in a city the size of Los Angeles, we're not even making a dent. But when you remember that only around 20 percent of Americans are weekly attenders in church—imagine if just 1 percent of that number did something similar each Christmas. It's such a simple thing to do, but if a tiny percentage of American Christians began their own "Craigslist Christmas," it would make a *major* impact—first, with the people helped, and second, in the way culture perceives us.

Kelly Corales is one example. A single mom of two, she had already told her kids there would be no Christmas that year when she stumbled across the ad on Craigslist. In a note to us, she wrote, "Just thinking of it brings tears to my eyes. It's a low point I can never ever forget." By offering to help her, not only were we able to erase her immediate Christmas need, but something just as profound happened. She wrote:

> At a time I was at my lowest financially and in a period when I had strayed away from God and the church, He sent me these people—Christians no less—to help me with Christmas and it was like my flame for Christ was relit. I knew it *had* to be God. Back in my car in the Target parking lot, I cried so hard and thanked God for blessing me even though I was so undeserving.

While reactions like this aren't totally surprising, since the moms are most directly impacted, more surprising are the reactions of the store employees. Even though our endeavors in the store are very understated, the staffers know something is up. At the particular Target we frequent, some employees even remember us from years past and warmly greet us. In a conversation one evening, a cashier asked me who we were, where we were from, and why we did this. When we told him, his response was, "Yeah, I don't go to church myself. But I've never seen people act this way with total strangers. That's very cool."

You may say that plenty of Christian charities are doing work just like this, and you'd be correct. Organizations like The Salvation Army, the US Marine Corps Reserve Toys for Tots, and a host of local church outreaches are impacting communities in remarkable ways. But one of the great tragedies of the twenty-first century is that for the most part, Christians have farmed out the hard work of the gospel. Because of nonprofit groups like Samaritan's Purse, WorldVision, Compassion International, and others, all we have to do is send a donation and then forget about it. We've largely forgotten the importance of each of us being the hand and heart of God.

We are robbing ourselves of the opportunity to learn to love unconditionally.

Those sponsorships and donations are important to large-scale charity organizations, and there's no question they have developed efficient programs to meet the needs of the homeless, the abused, men and women in prison, or those addicted to drugs and alcohol. You and I can't duplicate these remarkable programs.

But we also can't neglect doing what we can ourselves. It's one thing to financially support a Thanksgiving dinner on skid row, but it's another thing altogether to show up and serve.

What if our churches started filling the streets with individual Christians reaching out to neighbors in need—mowing the grass of a widow next door, painting the house of a retired couple down the street, or babysitting for the single mom in the apartment above you?

Certainly, it's messy. Sometimes at Craigslist Christmas, we experience one parent who is weepy and effusively grateful along with a spouse who is silent and unapproachable. Maybe they are too proud or too ashamed to show emotion or say a simple, "Thank you." And sometimes the widow next door is angry and ungrateful. Addicts often revert to their old ways.

But don't serve others simply to change *their* lives—do it to change *yours*.

> My idea of Christmas, whether old-fashioned or modern, is very simple: loving others. Come to think of it, why do we have to wait for Christmas to do that?
>
> —COMEDIAN BOB HOPE

Historian Robert Louis Wilken, in his excellent book *The Christians as the Romans Saw Them*, writes, "Some people initially joined the Christian sect because they found the figure of Jesus attractive, others because they were persuaded of the superiority of the Christian way of life by the behavior of a friend, others because they had married Christians."

In an American Christian culture—where our focus has been on church programs, corporate evangelistic outreaches, and other event-driven campaigns—we can't forget the power of being "persuaded of the superiority of the Christian way of life by the behavior of a friend." In fact, Wilken goes on to say, "One critic has hinted that the reason Christianity succeeded in making its way within the Roman world was due less to what Christians believed than to the way they lived."

We invite you and your friends to steal our idea of Craigslist Christmas. Better still, come up with your own ways to show love and empathy to a broken world all year long!

CHAPTER 11

APARTMENT LIFE

I hope churches will . . . take the risky path
of celebrating their members who do not go into
"full-time Christian service" but who serve
Christ full time in their own arena of culture.

ANDY CROUCH,
CULTURE MAKING

The Christian shoemaker does his duty
not by putting little crosses on the shoes
but by making good shoes.

ANONYMOUS

ONE OF THE MOST influential ministry outreaches we've ever encountered is The Barnabas Group. This organization, in cities across America, is designed to bring Christian business leaders together to hear presentations from innovative ministry outreaches in their area. If a business leader in the audience feels a strong connection to a particular ministry's or nonprofit's presentation, then he or she can offer financial support, business or leadership counsel, networking advice, and other ways to help the ministry grow or get to the next level.

Over the years, this organization has generated more than $500 million for Christian causes. It was at an Orange County event, hosted by our friends Jim and Suzy West, that we heard about Apartment Life.

In 1997, Stan Dobbs left a career in the computer industry and packed up for seminary in Fort Worth, Texas. While also working on staff at a church, he recognized the incredible numbers of singles and young couples living in apartments who reported feeling lonely and unable to connect with other people. It's one of the great ironies of our current culture: multiple families packed into a single building who don't know or rarely come in contact with each other. "Fifty percent of the population of Dallas lives in apartments," Stan said, "and yet the existing outreach strategies have been terribly ineffective in reaching apartment residents."

In the United States, two studies showed that 40 per cent of people say they're lonely, a figure that has doubled in 30 years. . . . Says Ami Rokach, a psychologist and lecturer at York University in Toronto, . . . 'Loneliness has been linked to depression, anxiety, interpersonal hostility, increased vulnerability to health problems, and even to suicide.'

—ELIZABETH RENZETTI, WRITING FOR *THE GLOBE AND MAIL*

Stan had an unusual idea. In 2000, he launched an organization called Apartment Life in downtown Fort Worth with the goal of penetrating the walls of massive apartment complexes with the message of the gospel. He created a concept he called Community Activities and Resident Services (CARES) teams. A team consists of either a married couple or two singles of the same gender, and they are given a free apartment for working eighty hours per month to assist the apartment complex management in building community and serving residents.

Stan's job is to sell the apartment owner on the idea that giving a free apartment to a Christian couple will be good for his or her bottom line. His goal is to convince the owner that in exchange for free rent, the couple's job is to create a better and more vibrant sense of community within the complex. To accomplish that, they become what some might call "chaplains" for the residents. They visit the sick, hold community events, set up basketball leagues, and throw pool parties—all designed to bring people together.

And it's worked. To date, there are more than one hundred

of these teams working to bring a stronger sense of community to people who would otherwise never know their next-door neighbor. And since these team members are Christian couples, spiritual conversations naturally happen.

Even though Apartment Life is driven by a Christian commitment, the apartment owners couldn't be more thrilled.

Complexes with a CARES team have a far lower turnover rate than other apartment complexes, which makes the owners very happy.

According to survey results from residents in the apartment communities utilizing the CARES teams:

- 88 percent believe that the "sense of community" is better or much better than in other apartments.
- And 48 percent indicated that the teams were an important or very important factor in their initial decision to lease.
- 65 percent indicated that the teams were an important or very important factor in their lease renewal decision.

And when it comes to sharing their Christian faith, Dobbs explained, "We basically put appropriate boundaries around our evangelism to make it palatable from a business perspective, and that's frankly the real value we've brought to the table in this whole genre of apartment ministry." As one CARES team member stated in a news article on the organization, "There's never been an activity that we've done where there's not been a spiritual conversation of some sort. Usually they'll see something different in your life and they'll ask you about it."

AN OPEN DOOR TO EVANGELISM

That open door to evangelism is what Apartment Life is all about. For our purposes, let's take a look at what Stan Dobbs is pioneering.

HE SAW A NEED

Dobbs saw a need that everyone—believers and unbelievers alike—agreed on: loneliness and lack of community. Had he gone to apartment owners and presented the need to reach people for Christ, he would have been kicked out straightaway. But by first addressing the issues apartment owners care about (low turnover rates and longer rental returns), Apartment Life found building owners to be enthusiastic partners.

HE DIDN'T LEAD WITH THE GOSPEL

The CARES teams don't hand out tracts or set up a gospel booth in the apartment lobby. They start by offering a hand during a move, bringing food for a sick resident, or sponsoring a pool party. It's the same proven missionary strategy that has worked for generations: develop a relationship first, and win people's trust.

In today's secular and highly skeptical world, *earning the right to be heard* matters. Remember that with all the power of the empire at his disposal, Roman emperor Julian was unable to destroy the growth of the Early Church because their *actions* spoke far more eloquently than their sermons. The Salvation Army has global credibility because their addiction treatment programs are among the finest in the world. Pastor Rick Warren is welcomed by government leaders because of the effective work he's done for HIV patients globally. Mercy Ships makes such a life-changing medical contribution that countries can't wait for the world's largest hospital ships to show up in their harbors.

HE GETS PROVEN RESULTS

President John Adams liked to say, "Facts are stubborn things." Even if you disagree with their mission, it's hard to argue with proven statistics that complexes with CARES teams have a lower turnover rate and happier tenants. An apartment owner may care little about spirituality, but he or she cares a great deal about the bottom line.

Because Mel Gibson's movie *The Passion of the Christ* was so successful at the box office, suddenly Hollywood studios who had never considered spiritual issues wanted to make more faith-based movies.

Because Celebrate Recovery has become such an effective addiction treatment program, people who would never consider coming to church are willing to enroll because it gets results.

Many churches across the country have such vibrant and high-quality school programs that parents who would never consider going to church can't wait to enroll their children.

God will permit what He hates to accomplish that
which He loves.

—AUTHOR AND MINISTRY LEADER
JONI EARECKSON TADA

Contrary to popular thinking, Christian missionary efforts
can turn things around for our culture and restore our credibility. Robert Woodberry from the University of North Carolina,
Chapel Hill did a landmark study of countries where Victorian-
era Christian missionaries worked. The current thinking
(particularly in academic circles) today is that Christian missionaries destroyed the local culture, religions, and overall were
a bad thing wherever they went. However, when Woodberry
studied the economic, educational, medical, familial, and other
markers in these countries, he discovered that the most successful African countries today were countries where Victorian-
era Christian missionaries worked. And the opposite was also
true: the countries today that are wracked by chaos, financial
instability, poor healthcare, and other negative markers were
countries Victorian-era Christian missionaries never went.
This remarkable study confirms that even though things may
be difficult right now, we actually can turn this around and
begin to restore our credibility in today's culture based on our
strategy.

OPENING THE DOOR TO THE GOSPEL

A diving accident left Joni Eareckson Tada, then seventeen
years old, a quadriplegic in a wheelchair. After two challenging years of rehabilitation, she emerged with a passion to help

others in similar situations. She founded Joni and Friends International Disability Center, which today is an international advocate for people with disabilities.

In visiting with Joni recently and touring their disability center with their outstanding leadership team, we were struck by her passion for leading people to Christ. But in spite of that priority, her team rarely leads with the gospel; instead, they lead with assisting people with disabilities and other challenges. For instance, one of their many programs reconditions old wheelchairs and makes them like new. Those wheelchairs are then distributed around the world to people too poor to afford one for themselves.

Each time, they present the gospel *after* presenting the wheelchair. Do secular governments care that she's sharing the gospel? Not much, apparently. They're lined up to receive more wheelchairs for their disabled poor. Even in Communist China, she's not allowed to share the gospel directly, but the country has embraced her wheelchair program. (And even though she's been barred from evangelism, her ministry *is* allowed to distribute copies of Joni's autobiography.)

By opening the door with something people want, the people become far more interested in a message that otherwise they'd never be interested in hearing.

THE POWER OF COMMUNITY

In his fascinating book *How the West Won: The Neglected Story of the Triumph of Modernity,* Rodney Stark makes what many would consider a startling statement: "Doctrines are of secondary importance in the initial decision to convert." While he mentions notable exceptions like the apostle Paul's Damascus Road experience, Stark's research indicates that for the vast majority of people, conversion is more about bringing one's religious behavior in line with family and friends—in other words, the community.

Creating a vibrant and welcoming community can be a compelling prerequisite for reaching people with the gospel. That's a significant reason Apartment Life works. Their first goal is to create community, because that opens the door to relationships, social acceptance, and potentially, a decision to receive Christ.

Consider all the other possibilities in your neighborhood where Christians can make a notable community impact: volunteering in senior centers, assisted living facilities, and after-school programs; becoming mall greeters; offering free Christmas wrapping or Christmas tree disposal; visiting shut-ins; doing yard work for the elderly; babysitting for young families and single parents; helping with bags and carts at the super market; doing trash cleanups, and so on.

Since she was a teenage girl, Jonathan's mom has tried to live each day with a simple goal—make each day count for eternity.

We're begging you to steal that and make it your credo too!

If we make a substantive contribution first, then eternal results will surely follow.

CHAPTER 12

FOSTER
THE (YOUNG) PEOPLE

We do not exist for ourselves alone.

THOMAS MERTON,
NO MAN IS AN ISLAND

Whoever receives one such child
in my name receives me.

MARK 9:37

IN THE ANCIENT WORLD, widows and orphans were a universal problem. Women's rights were virtually nonexistent, and without a husband, it was as if a woman didn't exist. In far too many cultures, widows were left to scavenge from the scraps society left over—that's, of course, if you lived in a culture that didn't execute you upon the death of your husband. Orphans were just as insignificant. War, pestilence, famine, disease, prostitution, rape, and a host of other scourges have done their best to make sure cultures always had a bumper crop of unwanted children.

For thousands of years, governments have debated what to do with abandoned children. Most of the time, politicians have done nothing or, worse, have either outright killed orphans or used them as a source of revenue by trafficking them as slaves. But amidst this human abyss, a bright ray of hope cut into the darkness—a curious and surprising little scripture:

> Religion that is pure and undefiled before God the Father is this: to visit orphans and widows in their affliction, and to keep oneself unstained from the world. (James 1:27)

Apparently, what the world throws away still matters to God.

From the earliest days of Christianity, the church has tried to do something to help the most vulnerable. As mentioned in an earlier chapter, it began with picking up children left to die of exposure. The overwhelming numbers soon led to orphanages.

THE FOUNDER OF FOSTER CARE

In the United States, the modern foster care system has all but eliminated the need for traditional orphanages. Just as orphanages were largely founded by the church, the idea for foster care was also developed by a Christian—Charles Loring Brace. In the mid-nineteenth century, there were about thirty thousand homeless or neglected children living in New York City alone. Brace decided to do something about it. Driven by the belief that these children should be raised in a Christian family (he felt farm families should be the priority choice), he sent thousands of these homeless children all across the country—mostly by train—to waiting families.

His organization was called the Children's Aid Society, and after his death in 1890, it was continued by his sons. The Children's Aid Society still exists today, based in New York City. Eventually, foster care in the United States transitioned to a combination of public and private agencies. On any given day, there are roughly 450,000 children in foster care.

Los Angeles County Department of Children and Family Services kept foster kids' money, audit says
—HEADLINE FROM THE *LOS ANGELES DAILY NEWS*

Unfortunately, Charles Brace would hardly recognize today's foster care program in America. While there are thousands of compassionate and dedicated foster care parents and workers across the country, today's headlines are regularly filled with stories of abuse, neglect, and corruption in the foster care system.

In our home city of Los Angeles, it's easy to find reports of financial mismanagement and neglect. The *Los Angeles Times* recently reported, "A longtime employee of the Los Angeles County Department of Children and Family Services has been fired after an internal affairs investigation concluded that he sexually propositioned foster children under his care." But the truth is, as bad as these individual stories are, the system doesn't work. Consider these national statistics:

- Only 54 percent of foster children earn a high school diploma.
- Only 2 percent earn a bachelor's degree or higher.
- 51 percent of foster care graduates are unemployed.
- 84 percent of foster care graduates become parents too soon, exposing their children to a repeated cycle of neglect and abuse.

According to the organization United Friends of the Children: "The lives of foster youth are disproportionately marked by violence. Some foster youth who have been removed from their families because of violence are retraumatized by violence or abuse while in foster care. For example, over 40 percent reported 'severe physical punishment' while in care. Additionally, 15 percent reported that they had been sexually abused while in foster care."

In some cities across this country the foster care system is a virtual catastrophe. While there are heroic pockets of social workers, government employees, and foster parents desperately trying to make a difference, in far too many places today, we are losing the battle.

But all is not lost.

There's a hero out there! A group of people who could fix it! After all, it's in their blood.

> Learn to do good; seek justice, correct oppression; bring justice to the fatherless, plead the widow's cause.
> (Isaiah 1:17)

Just as the Early Church began to transform the attitudes of grassroots Romans through taking in abandoned children, the modern American church could do something similar today with foster care. The premise is simple. With more than three hundred thousand Christian churches in America today, what if we took responsibility for the well-being of any foster child within a few miles of each church?

What would the response of the non-Christian culture be if that happened? You don't have to be a Christian to realize the enormity of the foster care challenges facing social service agencies, local governments, and ministry organizations today. To a secular culture that's looking for answers to these problems, how would it shift their perception of what Christianity is and how it can impact lives? Two kids per church would wipe out the foster care system entirely.

"Impossible," you say?

A MODEL THAT DOES IT RIGHT

A few years ago, we had the opportunity to visit a Christian non-profit organization in South Florida called 4KIDS. Originally launched by a local church (Calvary Chapel in Fort Lauderdale), 4KIDS recognized the growing problems with foster care throughout South Florida and decided to make a difference.

4KIDS is focused on newborns to seventeen-year-olds, which is essentially every child in Broward County brought into the child welfare system after being removed from their families due to abuse, neglect, or abandonment. Through their program called SafePlace, once a police officer or child welfare worker removes a child from an unsafe home, they are immediately taken to SafePlace where they are provided food, shelter, and supervision by trained, qualified, and screened staff members and volunteers. As one of their staff members told us, their goal is to help these children learn to trust and laugh again.

SafePlace is one of the only programs of its kind in the state of Florida, and it is open 24 hours a day, 365 days a year. A decade ago, the foster care system in South Florida was overcrowded and in need of restructure. SafePlace 4KIDS was launched in the face of a need for more foster homes, and it didn't take long for people in the community to respond.

Child placement agencies throughout Broward and Palm Beach Counties work with 4KIDS to place these children in a foster care family or a family-style home that allows siblings to stay together while they await placement in a foster home or with a family member.

Think about this for a minute:

A *Christian* organization, founded by a local church,
is now the go-to place for law enforcement and
social services for an entire geographical area of the state.

But 4KIDS's involvement with these children doesn't end when they work through the system. With most foster care programs, at age eighteen, young men and women are simply handed a check as they exit the foster care network. But a significant number of them have no family members, mentors, or anyone to help them reach educational, career, or personal goals. So 4KIDS developed an Independent Living program that fills these gaps by giving these young adults a roof over their heads and mentors to help guide them during this next stage of their lives.

4KIDS has the respect and support of vast numbers of citizens in that community. When we attended a yearly fundraiser, we noticed that it wasn't just Christians who came to support the effort. People from all walks of life, all religious backgrounds, and all political perspectives were crowding that hotel ballroom to see the results and pledge their financial support.

450 THOUSAND FOSTER KIDS, 300 THOUSAND US CHURCHES

What if every church in America got serious about solving this problem? What if in every church, members were found to take in these children, other members were found to help financially, and still other members supported and nurtured the adoptive families? If we wanted to, we could wipe out the entire foster care system in one year.

What kind of impact would that make on the next generation of young people?

The church can continue to farm out the problem to social service agencies and the government—or, like the founders of 4KIDS, we can decide that these children deserve much better. If the Bible's definition of pure religion is visiting orphans in their affliction (James 1:27), then this would be a great place to start.

CHAPTER 13

WHAT DRIVES
YOU CRAZY?

Your ministry is in your misery.

BISHOP T. D. JAKES

Why didn't you come sooner?

SONIA, A SURVIVOR OF SEX TRAFFICKING

CHRISTINE CARYOFYLLIS was adopted at birth and raised attending a Greek Orthodox Church in Australia. Upon graduating from Sydney University, she enrolled in Hillsong College, founded by Brian Houston of the internationally known Hillsong Church in Sydney, where she pursued training in preaching and evangelism. It was at Bible college that she met the love of her life, Nick Caine, and they were married in 1996.

Christine went from serving as a youth leader in her local church, to directing a statewide youth ministry, to eventually starting Equip & Empower ministries with her husband Nick. While remaining a key part of Hillsong Church's leadership team as a traveling evangelist, she has spent the last 25 years building the local church on a global scale through preaching and teaching around the world.

It was while she was traveling on her way to a women's conference in Greece that Christine became aware of a global injustice that impacts millions of people throughout the world today: human trafficking.

In response, Christine and Nick founded the A21 Campaign in 2008 with the lofty but determined goal of abolishing slavery everywhere, forever. In the midst of full-time ministry and a busy travel schedule, Caine and her team took on the 150.2 billion dollar global human trafficking industry.

Nicole Partridge has written for *Charisma* magazine about the beginning of A21:

"I was transiting through Thessaloniki Airport when I noticed posters of young girls and women who had gone missing, some as young as 6," [Caine] recalls. Asking the pastor accompanying her some questions, she discovered the girls had been trafficked.

That night in her hotel, Caine says God clearly spoke to her through Luke 10. "While I was so troubled by what I had seen, I was still thinking, *I am the Good Samaritan,*" she explains. "But then God clearly said to me, 'No . . . you are the Levite and the priest in the story who walked to the other side.'"

Today, A21 has thirteen offices in twelve countries and focuses on reaching the vulnerable through prevention, awareness, and education, rescuing victims through working closely with law enforcement and assisting in the prosecutions of traffickers, and restoring survivors through holistic aftercare and repatriation assistance. One of their largest awareness campaigns, Walk For Freedom, is held in more than fifty countries each year, and reaches tens of millions of people

They began their work in Greece, which is considered a gateway country into Western Europe for trafficking. They have established a national hotline, which has resulted in a 127 percent increase of human trafficking reporting, and resulted in the recovery of 111 victims of human trafficking in 2016 alone. They have assisted in the conviction of dozens of traffickers, with prison sentences resulting in hundreds of years of prison and millions of dollars in fines.

Many of the young girls that Christine, Nick, and their

team at A21 rescue are teenagers. During a time when they should be finishing high school, talking about boys, or hanging out with friends, these women are lured into sexual slavery under the pretense of a better life.

Most of these women begin life trapped in poverty in countries like Romania, Moldova, Ukraine, Bulgaria, Russia, Nigeria, or Uzbekistan. They're often approached by well-dressed and attractive strangers telling them stories of opportunities that seem too good to be true for these girls facing limited options: becoming a nanny for rich families in Italy, waitressing in nice restaurants in France, or studying in the United Kingdom. But as they eventually find out, these opportunities are just that—made-up stories.

Once they girls say yes, they're taken away from everything they know, beaten, drugged, and forced into the sex industry. At the beginning, they are beaten and raped for weeks on end until the girls withdraw to a dark place inside and eventually give up. Once submissive, these women are forced into sex with strangers up to sixty times a day. Their passports and identification documents are taken, so they have no way of escape, no one to turn to, and no hope. After years of this abuse, any sense of healing and restoration is nearly impossible.

And that's why A21 matters.

WHAT CAN WE LEARN
FROM A21'S STORY?

With teams on the ground collecting intelligence about the trafficking industry, freedom centers caring for survivors, collaboration with governments and law enforcement to increase victim identification, and more, A21 has gone to the heart of one of the darkest and most insidious evils of this century.

We tell Christine's story because it exemplifies three truths.

NOTHING HAPPENS UNTIL SOMETHING MOVES

When they began, neither Christine nor Nick was an expert in the issue of human trafficking. In fact, it would be fair to say they knew little more than what they saw occasionally on the evening news. After all, Christine had been trained as an evangelist, not a social worker. But they decided to act. With courage and determination, they founded an organization, that, within less than a decade, has facilities in place, teams on the ground in multiple countries, and is working at ground zero of the human trafficking industry.

Great impact doesn't necessarily happen because you're an expert, bring years of experience, or have an academic degree. It happens because someone acts. As Albert Einstein once said, "Nothing happens until something moves."

LEAD WITH ACTION

If you've ever heard Christine share the gospel, you know she's passionate about evangelism. However, A21 is not registered as a Christian ministry, but rather as an NGO (non-governmental organization). This allows them to work alongside governments and in schools in nations around the world, and accomplish their immediate job: to rescue victims of human trafficking. Just like the story of the Good Samaritan that started it all for Christine, leading with action is a key part of the work of the gospel.

Right belief or behavior was never a prerequisite for spending time with Jesus. When the religious leaders dragged a woman into the streets to stone her for adultery, Jesus loved her and protected her first, before (and possibly without) any change on her part. We are either the ones holding the stones or the ones fighting to protect the woman on the ground. Jesus's example is clear.

—C. M. JOYNER, WRITING FOR *RELEVANT* MAGAZINE

What most governmental and legal authorities in various countries care about is, "Does it work?" And A21 works.

RESULTS CAN'T BE DENIED

As with Craigslist Christmas, Apartment Life, and 4KIDS, positive results will often bridge differences in beliefs. In the case of A21, the local authorities marvel at A21's success. As a result, the astonished civil authorities in multiple countries have not only welcomed their help but rolled out the red carpet. In countries where red tape can be a nightmare for everyone else, A21 has been able to sign formal agreements with governments, and in many cases, a bureaucratic Red Sea has been parted.

Around the world, A21 partners with the authorities in training identifiers and responding when a survivor is rescued with holistic care and services. In the United States, they've assisted the FBI and state law enforcement by providing resources to share with those identified as victims. In Greece, they trained more than 688 law enforcement officers in 2014 alone, with 76 percent voluntarily signing up to be on the A21 Task Force. In Thailand, they have partnered with the Royal Thai Police's Thailand Internet Crimes Against Children Task Force to open a Child Advocacy Center that assists in child forensic interviews with a multidisciplinary team approach to allegations of child abuse.

> If it wasn't for the training that you provided to my police unit, we would not have known how to deal with the case of human trafficking that we recently had. Thank you for the great work that you are doing.
>
> —CAPTAIN PETROPOULOUS, GREEK LAW ENFORCEMENT OFFICER, IN A LETTER TO A21

Why would this Australian woman and her husband go to such extremes to help people few others care about? Why are they making such an effort to love and protect those they don't even know? Why are they willing to fight such a massive evil industry? Why are they willing to take on the enormous financial risk?

When asked about her legacy, Christine Caine said, "Wherever she went, there was little light, but when she left, there was no darkness." That, Caine says, "would be the ultimate legacy."

SO, WHAT DRIVES *YOU* CRAZY?

The title of this chapter is the question you could be asking yourself: "What drives *you* crazy?" It may be a big question like human trafficking, hunger, homelessness, or abuse. Or it might be something far smaller—perhaps a poorly led program or underfunded outreach at your church, the lonely kids next door because their single mom is working two jobs, a coworker who's going through treatment for cancer, or a friend who's struggling with alcohol or drug addiction.

Whatever it is, it's not the size of the task that's important. As theologian R. C. Sproul has written, "God can use the smallest words that we speak, the smallest service that we give, and bring a kingdom out of it."

Sometimes your great calling in life isn't a passion or dream. Sometimes it's something you hate, or something that drives you crazy. Sometimes, as Bishop T. D. Jakes says, "Your ministry is in your misery."

CHAPTER 14

THE DROP BOX

The hallmark of a healthy society has always been measured by how it cares for the disadvantaged.

AUTHOR AND MINISTRY LEADER
JONI EARECKSON TADA

The ideas that shape politics and a culture
are rarely advanced by argument.
Rather, they are advanced by the stories
that shape our imaginations.

WARREN COLE SMITH AND JOHN STONESTREET,
RESTORING ALL THINGS

A FEW YEARS AGO, we attended a screening of the film *The Drop Box* in Los Angeles. Directed by Brian Ivie, the documentary film tells the remarkable story of Lee Jong-rak, pastor of Jusarang (God's Love) Community Church in Seoul, South Korea. Worldwide, millions of children are abandoned at birth, and the reasons are pretty similar everywhere—birth defects, unwanted pregnancy, teen mothers, poverty, abuse, or social and family pressures. But in South Korea, because of a strict social code and the humiliation associated with living outside social norms, the problem is especially acute—and it's growing.

In many cases, the unwanted child is simply left to die in an abandoned alley or street corner or dumped in a trash bin. But occasionally they're left on someone's doorstep. When some of those unwanted newborns started being placed on Pastor Lee's church steps, he decided to take action. He and his wife, spurred by their Christian faith and the experience of raising a son with extreme disabilities, began to take in these children. Because of the long, cold winters in South Korea, he eventually built a "drop box" into the front wall of the church. With a door that opens from the outside as well as the inside, it's like a baby-sized drawer, complete with light bulb, heater, and a loud bell that alerts his family when a baby is placed in the box.

It wasn't long before the bell started sounding on a regular basis.

Today, Pastor Lee's family and a small group of volunteers provide a loving home for more than a dozen mildly to severely disabled children at a time. Over the years, they have saved hundreds of abandoned newborns.

Because of the potential embarrassment for mothers and their desire for secrecy, there are problems—and plenty of critics. Some say the "baby box" actually encourages mothers to give up their children, but a look at the history of the city confirms abandonment has been happening for generations. Despite the criticism, enormous cost, overwhelming amount of work, and the lack of any government funding—Pastor Lee and his family continue.

Night after night, Pastor Lee stays up listening for the alarm. When a new baby arrives, he races downstairs, bundles up the child, and prays. Then he and his wife begin the tedious task of filling out mountains of paperwork to have the child examined at a hospital or placed in an orphanage. Since there is rarely any record of the birth, even simple hospital visits can be a serious challenge.

What happens when the child is too severely disabled for an orphanage or state home? Pastor Lee's family takes them in. It is difficult and demanding work beyond the pale for the majority of people—especially those who aren't driven by the same spiritual motivation that drives Pastor Lee. But exactly because of that extraordinary calling and the difference he is making, both Christian and secular audiences flocked to see the film.

The Drop Box was a remarkable opportunity for Christians to share their faith.

After all, what's easier than inviting someone to see a movie? When we attended the screening in Los Angeles, the theater was packed, and as we left we heard conversation after conversation about Pastor Lee, the passion that drives him, and questions like, "Why would anyone sacrifice so much?" After seeing a story like Pastor Lee's, people who would never consider attending church are not only fascinated but eager to discuss the spiritual and moral implications of working with these desperate children.

It's worth noting that *The Hollywood Reporter* (the secular journal of the entertainment industry) was enthusiastic about the film:

> [The director] Ivie himself was transformed by the making of the film. He grew up going to church on Christmas and Easter and considering himself a Christian "because I didn't smoke cigarettes and I watched Fox News with my mom. It was a decorative label." But witnessing Lee's sacrifice and compassion for the abandoned children changed his perspective.

"These kids were helpless," he says, "and I realized I was broken and helpless too, and I also needed to be rescued."

Ivie actually went to South Korea to make a different movie, but once he met Pastor Lee and saw the work he and his team were doing, he changed his plans, produced *The Drop Box,* and in the process, dedicated his life to Christ.

The Hollywood Reporter review continues:

> Because of Focus' involvement, *The Drop Box* has been taken up by the pro-life movement, but Ivie regards attempts to politicize his documentary with some ambivalence. "I get why there's support from that community, but the reality is, people don't respond to agendas," says the Southern California native, now at work on his second feature, a narrative film about the 1960s Jesus movement. "[The documentary] is just showing one man who stood up and said, 'Please don't throw anyone away. I'll take you in and I will embrace your suffering.'
>
> "That's what I hope people do in response," Ivie says. "Instead of screaming at mothers on Facebook, I hope they say, 'Your life matters, and I will open up my life to your difficulty.'"

The question is, had the film's director encountered an anti-abortion protester, an activist, or someone leading a boycott rather than someone doing the difficult work of Pastor Lee, would he have been as compelled to commit his life to Christ? Probably not.

A Christian pastor living out his faith in the same way as the Early Church did, coupled with a transformed filmmaker with a passion to tell the story, generated a glowing report in a secular entertainment magazine seen by the most important decision makers in the industry.

If that's not a witness, we're not sure what is.

We have to show the world we have a better plan.

It's not enough to complain in the newspaper, hold up signs, or write an angry blog. We have to support pregnancy centers, counsel pregnant moms, and be there financially as well.

Keep in mind, the Early Church baffled the Romans and turned the tide of history to a significant degree over this very issue. But it wasn't complaining, holding protest signs, or marches that turned the tide, it was individual families going out at night and taking in abandoned infants who were dying of exposure. It was bringing them into their families and raising them as their own. And it was other members of the church who supported them financially.

In his book *Onward: Engaging the Culture Without Losing the Gospel,* Russell Moore summed it up well:

The kingdom of God turns the Darwinist narrative of
the survival of the fittest upside down (Acts 17:6-7).

When the church honors and cares for the vulnerable among us, we are not showing charity. We are simply recognizing the way the world really works, at least in the long run. The child with Down syndrome on the fifth row from the back in your church, he's not a "ministry project." He's a future king of the universe. The immigrant woman who scrubs toilets every day on hands and knees, and can barely speak enough English to sing along with your praise choruses, she's not a problem to be solved. She's a future queen of the cosmos, a joint-heir with Christ.

CHAPTER 15

RADICAL HUMILITY

The real test of a saint is not one's willingness
to preach the gospel, but one's willingness to do
something like washing the disciples' feet—that is,
being willing to do those things that seem unimportant
in human estimation but count as everything to God.

OSWALD CHAMBERS,
MY UTMOST FOR HIS HIGHEST

Jesus did not say that the whole world
should go to church.
But He did say that the church
should go to the whole world.

PASTOR GREG LAURIE

HE DIDN'T TELL ANYONE who he really was.

He just applied for the job, showed up, and quietly did the work. Weekend after weekend, he cleaned toilets, washed dishes, and bussed tables. And during that time, his heart changed.

For months, his secret was safe. Finally, someone on staff discovered that when he wasn't at the bar, this "janitor" was actually a millionaire! And a Christian! Everyone was stunned. Why had he done it?

French philosopher Blaise Pascal said, "There are only two kinds of men: the righteous who think they are sinners and the sinners who think they are righteous." This Christian friend of ours is a perfect example of that quote. Knowing in his heart he had always harbored negative feelings about members of the gay community, he did something radical—he applied to be a part-time janitor on weekends at a local gay bar.

The owners and the patrons were surprised, to say the least. Wanting to know why he cleaned restrooms at a gay bar, they put him on the spot. He didn't preach or lecture; he simply explained that he was a follower of Jesus and wanted to learn to be a servant.

That last line is important and is worth repeating:

**He didn't preach or lecture; he simply explained
that he was a follower of Jesus
and wanted to learn to be a servant.**

The patrons of that bar were not ready for that response. Over the years they had seen the judgmental side of Christianity through criticism, elections, pickets, and petitions. But the *servant* side of Christianity was unfamiliar territory.

It made an impact. As our friend told his story about how the experience cleaning restrooms changed *him*, it also began to transform how the patrons of that bar looked at *Christians*.

SERVICE CONQUERS
JUDGMENT

Novelist Kurt Vonnegut was an avowed "freethinker," but by some accounts he was nearly obsessed with the life of Jesus. In his volume of essays called *A Man Without a Country*, he brought up the Christian propensity to emphasize judgment over grace: "For some reason, the most vocal Christians among us never mention the Beatitudes. But, often with tears in their eyes, they demand that the Ten Commandments be posted on public buildings. And of course that's Moses, not Jesus. I haven't heard one of them demand that the Sermon on the Mount, the Beatitudes, be posted anywhere."

Certainly, Old Testament law is foundational to understanding our relationship to God. But when it comes to touching people in need—and hopefully transforming their lives—Jesus's example is the model we must follow to change others.

The Son of God became a man to enable men to become sons of God.

—C. S. LEWIS, *MERE CHRISTIANITY*

It's hard to imagine anything more humbling than the God of the universe lowering Himself to become a mortal man. A God who knows everything, sees everything, and is eternal and all-powerful allowing Himself to be caged in a frail human body with its limitations and restraints is nearly impossible to fathom. From that moment, however, humility became *the essence* of the Christian faith.

Because Jesus humbled Himself for us, it is our duty, obligation, and joy to humble ourselves as well. But to adjust ourselves into a radically humble lifestyle to escape the clutches of That Other God, the question we must ask ourselves is this:

Have we lived so long worshipping our own egos that we've lost our ability— *perhaps even our desire—* **to humble ourselves as Christ did?**

The first question that the priest asked, the first question that the Levite asked was, "If I stop to help this man, what will happen to me?" But then the Good Samaritan came by, and he reversed the question: "If I do not stop to help this man, what will happen to him?"

—MARTIN LUTHER KING JR., "I'VE BEEN TO THE MOUNTAINTOP" SPEECH

The power of our faith comes from simply serving the culture that surrounds us. Orphanages, universities, hospitals, homeless shelters, and so forth. History has shown that our greatest impact on the world has come from remarkable acts of service in communities like these.

Nobody gets a blessing if they have cold feet and nobody ever got saved while they had a toothache!

—WILLIAM BOOTH, COFOUNDER OF THE SALVATION ARMY

THE SALVATION ARMY

When we think of humility, we often think about William and Catherine Booth. William was born in Nottingham, England, in 1829, and he became a Christian as a teenager. He felt called to the ministry in the Methodist Church, and although he had opportunities to pastor a local congregation, he felt a stronger calling to work at the very lowest and darkest levels of society.

During the Victorian age, that meant ministry on the streets, to the those bound by poverty, alcohol, abuse, and much more. Alcoholism, prostitution, and child labor were particularly pernicious during this time. Booth realized that simply preaching the gospel wouldn't transport people out of their desperate circumstances, so he began organizing soup kitchens and homeless shelters.

That was his congregation, and that's where people's lives were transformed.

Though many received Christ through his work, he faced a new challenge. Because of their poverty, their past, and their circumstances, these new converts weren't being accepted into the churches. At the time, Victorian-era churches were steeped in rigid social layers, so without the support of organized churches the Booths launched their own organization.

It was a remarkable vision that was totally focused on outcasts—the most desperate men and women who had no other option or opportunity. They proclaimed their message on street corners and brought the gospel to thousands who would have never experienced the love and forgiveness of Jesus. They called it the Salvation Army.

The ministry grew over the years, and in spite of extraordinary opposition at times, the Salvation Army has become the largest ministry and social service agency in the world. It remains true to its mission, and in cities and towns across the United States and around the globe, you'll still find Salvation Army outposts dedicated to the homeless, those wracked by drugs and alcohol, orphaned and abused children, single mothers, and anyone else in immediate need.

And in those places, you'll also find Salvation Army churches boldly preaching the gospel. William and Catherine Booth never stopped their ministry to the lowest levels of society and never sought notoriety. More, they lived in the same places they ministered and spent their lives on the front lines of need.

William and Catherine Booth founded the Salvation Army in humility, and that attitude makes it one of the most effective ministry organizations in the world. Which is good, because sadly, some things never change. The Salvation Army was founded to reach out to sexually exploited young girls, the homeless, and those whose lives were destroyed by alcohol, and after 150 years, those needs still exist.

When we learned the story of the janitor in the gay bar and studied the lives of William and Catherine Booth, we thought, *What if millions of Christians suddenly became dedicated to a lifestyle of radical humility? What if we served—not for a promotion, recognition, or even the opportunity to share our faith— and did so in unexpected places?*

For millions of nonbelievers, it would be astonishing.

What if we served simply because Jesus commands us to do it?

If we are to better the future we must disturb the present.

—CATHERINE BOOTH, COFOUNDER
OF THE SALVATION ARMY

NOT PATIENTS BUT FRIENDS

One of our favorite stories about leaving self-interest behind is the story of Canadian Jean Vanier. As a young man, and despite plans to join the British Navy, Vanier was compelled by the gospel to work with the poor. He said, "Because I believed in the Gospel values, I felt called to leave the navy to follow Jesus. For me to follow Jesus was to announce the good news to the poor."

At that point, he moved to Paris and began studying with

a Dominican priest, Father Thomas Philippe. Vanier was brilliant, and he earned a doctorate on Aristotelian ethics from the Catholic Institute of Paris in 1962. His future was bright—that is, until his mentor, Father Thomas, became the chaplain at an institution for the mentally disabled in Trosly-Breuil.

After a single visit, Jean understood his real purpose and calling.

"I discovered this world," Vanier said later. "People locked up in institutions. Parents feeling ashamed, pained." One report indicates that at an institution near Paris, he saw eighty men locked up in a building meant for forty. Abuse was everywhere. Violence was common. In one town, he found a teenager chained inside a garage.

In those days throughout Europe (and most other places) the mentally ill were an inconvenience at best, and at worst, simply forgotten. "Hellhole" would be a nice description of most mental institutions of the time, and in many cases, well-intentioned therapy programs did little to improve matters. Keep in mind this attitude came from a history of institutionalization where, in some countries, the public could buy tickets to watch the insane just for amusement.

Vanier was devastated. At the time, there was little the state or local government would offer, so he purchased a small house and invited two mentally disabled men, Raphael Simi and Philippe Seux, to come live with him—not as inmates or patients but as friends.

That's worth repeating: *Not as patients but as friends.*

That was in 1964. Since then, L'Arche communities have opened in 147 countries, including throughout Europe, India, Canada, Mexico, Honduras, Egypt, and Zimbabwe. They are all dedicated to the belief that life matters, and even the most severely disabled—mentally and physically—deserve to live with dignity.

> Self-interest is but the survival of the animal in us.
> Humanity only begins for man with self-surrender.
> —SWISS POET AND CRITIC HENRI-FRÉDÉRIC AMIEL

Since then, the culture has noticed. Although a dedicated priest, Vanier doesn't lead with his faith. Instead, he leads with his commitment to servanthood, and that has generated enormous attention. Although Vanier doesn't do it for recognition, he has received numerous awards, including Companion of the Order of Canada and the Legion of Honour (France). Vanier was awarded the Templeton Prize in recognition of his advocacy for people with disabilities and exploring the issue of helping the weak and vulnerable. In the words on the prize itself, he was honored as an individual who has made "an exceptional contribution to affirming life's spiritual dimension."

As of this writing, Jean Vanier still makes his home in the original L'Arche community of Trosly-Breuil, France. In a recent story on his life in the *Wall Street Journal*, the newspaper asked him: "But what about those who can't take years off to serve?"

He responded, "Try and find somebody who is lonely. And when you go to see them, they will see you as the messiah. Go and visit a little old lady who has no friends or family. Bring her flowers. People say, 'but that's nothing.' It is nothing—but it's also everything." He added, "It always begins with small little things. It all began in Bethlehem. That was pretty small."

> We are all called to do, not extraordinary things, but very ordinary things, with an extraordinary love that flows from the heart of God.
>
> —JEAN VANIER, *COMMUNITY AND GROWTH*

CHAPTER 16

WHY DO WE CRY
AT FUNERALS?

A good man leaves an inheritance
to his children's children.

PROVERBS 13:22 NKJV

If anyone at my funeral has a long face,
I'll never speak to him again!

COMEDIAN STAN LAUREL

HERE'S A FASCINATING question for Christians to ponder:

Why do we cry at funerals?

When we read the multitude of scriptures about resurrection and eternal life, do we really believe them? Sure we miss Uncle Bob, but the truth is Uncle Bob just stepped across the threshold . . . into *eternity*! So why are we dressing in black, weeping, and grieving at his funeral?

It's time we get this party started!

Imagine for a moment you are one of our fictitious Uncle Bob's friends from work, so you don't know a ton about his personal life. You and a fellow coworker pull up to the church to attend Bob's memorial service. You're both wearing dark outfits, and, walking into that sanctuary, you're feeling pretty somber. After all, your friend Bob died.

But you walk in and you're met with a calypso band, streamers, balloons, dancing, singing, and general whoop-whoopness. Everyone else in the church is dressed in bright colors, having a blast and celebrating as if it's happy hour on a tropical beach. When they finally get around to the "memorial" part of the service, it's like a roast—all the speakers share stories of Uncle Bob and his joyful life as a Christian. And it doesn't feel like Bob is gone at all; rather, it feels like they're about to introduce him to speak next.

That's because, while he's gone from us, Bob's not dead. Bob cheated death!

When Bob's crazy fun party funeral is finally over, you get back in the car with your work friend. What's the conversation?

While you roll that one around in your head, understand just how countercultural that scene would be. We live in a country today where the physical reality of death isn't really experienced or addressed. Gone are the days of three-day wakes and open casket funerals. Death is out there waiting, of course, but it's a subject that is avoided at all costs.

But what if Christians became known as the people who celebrate departures from this world? What if we made our memorial services bigger and better than the best wedding you've ever attended? How would that impact the culture's perception of how seriously we believe what the Bible says? And what would it say about heaven?

Understand that this isn't to make light of real grief, especially in cases of senseless or premature deaths like that of children. There are certain cases where a solemn ceremony is appropriate and important. But the current lifespan in America is now almost eighty, so thankfully those special cases are fairly rare these days.

"THIS ISN'T LIKE ANY FUNERAL I'VE EVER ATTENDED"

Lois was a widow living in Las Vegas. For years she had lived a full and contented life, enjoying her retirement with her grandchildren, church, and friends. The death of her husband of almost fifty years left her with an aching heart, but she was a powerful example of her faith to those around her.

During a visit by her daughter one weekend, Lois pulled her aside and said, "I just want you to know that I've been praying about it, and I've made my peace with Jesus and am ready to go to heaven. I don't want you to be afraid. I want you to be at peace knowing that I am with our heavenly Father."

As Lois was in her seventies and in good health for her age, her daughter didn't think much about it. But just four days after returning home, she received a call from the Las Vegas Police Department informing her that a close friend had just found her mom dead in her bed. She had passed away in her sleep peacefully.

At the funeral, her Jewish physician stood up and shared how Lois had told him she was praying to die this way, and he wanted to attend the funeral so that everyone would know that she was at peace. He admitted that he was astonished that this was exactly how she died. He had never seen such a direct answer to prayer in all his life.

Not only did God answer Lois's prayer, but even in death she was still leading others to know Jesus.

Well, the funeral was a joyous event! The reception afterward was filled with family members recounting great stories about her life, her marriage, and her family. At one point in the evening, one of Lois's longtime friends said, "This isn't like any funeral I've ever attended."

DO WE REALLY KNOW
WHAT ETERNITY MEANS?

Author and speaker Francis Chan has the best illustration of eternity that we've ever seen. During his message, he brings out a very long rope. We're talking *long*! The rope winds around and around the stage, and it eventually runs off the stage to who knows where. At one end of the rope is a one-inch section painted red. The rest of the rope is white. In his talk, Chan explains that the short, one-inch red section of the rope is our life, while the rest of the rope is eternity. His point is clear: we spend so much time planning and worrying about such a short span, and we give remarkably little thought to what really counts—eternity.

Francis Chan and his rope can't be everywhere, so the question becomes, how can the Christian community share with today's culture the significance and the joyful possibilities of eternity?

MAYBE IT'S TIME TO CELEBRATE

We do it by acting on what we believe, by putting the "fun" into funerals. We do it by throwing memorial services that don't just honor a well-lived life but instead party like it's a graduation into the *rest* of life!

People will take notice.

And when they ask questions, we'll be there to graciously share what the Bible says about our relationship with an eternal God. But it can't be sporadic or occasional. To be effective, it should be common. Everyone in the Christian community needs to make celebrating our "homegoings" a priority.

Today, we don't think twice about hiring a professional to help us plan a wedding. But what if we hired a professional to help us plan our funerals? What if the Christian community suddenly became known as the people who celebrate funerals? And we really mean *party*! What if we did it so often—and so big—that people started to notice?

And what if the culture started asking why?

CHAPTER 17

PERSECUTION
IS THE NEW BLACK

Do everything without complaining and arguing,
so that no one can criticize you.
Live clean, innocent lives as children of God,
shining like bright lights in a world full
of crooked and perverse people.

PHILIPPIANS 2:14–15 NLT

Is Jesus worth it?

MISSIONARY NIK RIPKEN

NO BOOK LIKE THIS would be complete without addressing the potential ramification if we return wholeheartedly to serving God—namely, the return of persecution. One of the primary reasons we abandoned the true God in favor of That Other God was to sidestep that very possibility. But faithfulness and persecution go hand-in-hand and always have. So we can be sure that if a renewed Christian commitment comes to our country, persecution will be in vogue again too.

The truth is, many of these serious issues are happening because we've failed in our witness. As our perception dims in the surrounding culture, the idea that Christian belief makes a positive contribution—or even makes sense—dims with it. If we're not living out our principles in the culture every day on an internal, personal level, then it's easy to see why the culture stops noticing. And when that happens, it becomes easier and easier to marginalize the Christian faith on a much bigger and more public scale.

> Once abolish the God, and the Government becomes the God.
>
> —JOURNALIST AND LAY THEOLOGIAN G. K. CHESTERTON

It's essentially a domino effect. As we individually become less like Jesus and assimilate into the culture, people around us lose sight of the gospel's impact and begin replacing it with secular sources. For instance, when Christianity loses its preeminent place in the culture, it's perfectly natural for people to seek moral authority from others—politicians, intellectuals, political parties, celebrities, self-help gurus, or the state. When the church becomes less important, people look to secular organizations that can deal with personal and social needs. We believe this is a significant reason for the explosion in "cause marketing" today.

In modern America, there have been some hostile actions against the church, like cities that used imminent domain laws to take land from churches to build big box stores, and the mayor of a major American city who demanded all pastors within city limits turn over any sermons on homosexuality or LGBT issues for her review, and cases of universities expelling Christian clubs from the campus unless they allow nonbelievers in leadership. But in most of these sorts of cases, while they are a challenge, a good team of lawyers can usually do the trick, so they become exceptions rather than the rule.

But if adherence to the S⁷ Mysteries of surrender, Scripture, submission, service, sacrifice, simplicity, and suffering reinvigorates Christians to a holiness not seen in generations in America, then you can be sure that the weeds of outright persecution will blossom as well—both outside and inside the church.

"*Inside* the church?" you say? Indeed. Historically, those who drift from the church herd to seek holiness—and then encourage others to follow their lead—have been fiercely attacked. And when repentant men and women realize the extent of their own home church's creeping adoration of That Other God, the battle lines will be drawn. Something will have to give. One cannot serve two masters. The immediate reaction of those who still worship that idol will be anger, and then overreach in their attempts to bring everyone back to the status quo.

But in cases of persecution from both inside and outside the church, the methods of our response should be the same.

NEVER GIVE UP ON SEEKING
PERSONAL HOLINESS

Great movements don't always start from the top; they often start from the bottom with our own internal transformation. Often, when we're confronted with interference, possible punishment, or intimidation, we throw our hands in the air and give up.

But we forget that our story began at the bottom.

Jesus refused to exercise earthly power (surrender), wasn't rich (sacrifice), and didn't call an army at His disposal (submission). He spoke the truth (Scripture), washed His disciples' feet (service), had no place to call His home (simplicity), and was eventually crucified (suffering).

And in that process, He transformed the world.

Likewise, the apostles and the Early Church had little in terms of earthly influence, but what they taught became the dominant religious faith of the Western world. They acted individually, but they also acted as one. Each person understood that if he or she would commit their own lives to becoming authentic examples of the teachings of Jesus, it would change their families, their friends, and those around them.

That type of thinking started a revolution.

If individual Christians in America allow these S⁷ Mysteries to go deep into their spirit and start humbly acting on their renewed convictions, some will be offended—but more will be inspired.

CHRISTIANS NEED TO STAY
RIGHT WHERE THEY ARE

When confronted by attack, either at work or even at church, the goal of the attack is silence or separation. Your attacker wants you to shut up and/or leave. So don't!

We must remain there to *graciously* set the example.

Right now, there are committed Christians who have chosen to engage the secular and risky worlds of politics, entertainment, business, sports, technology, academia, the arts, and more, and they're making a real difference. There are Christians working in the creative departments of television networks, helping shape the direction of prime-time television programming. There are Christians in government trying to adhere to higher principles. There are Christians in the world of technology working every day to use digital tools to improve humanity.

What if they all disengaged because of persecution? Would the world be a better or worse place?

After World War II, looking back on the rise of Nazi Germany, physicist Albert Einstein confessed to *Time* magazine:

Only the Church stood squarely across the path of Hitler's campaign for suppressing the truth. I had never any special interest in the Church before, but now I feel a great affection and admiration because the Church alone has had the courage and persistence to stand for intellectual truth and moral freedom. I am forced thus to confess that what I once despised, I now praise unreservedly.

Speaking the truth about the Nazi danger to civilization cost many—such as Dietrich Bonhoeffer—their lives. So speaking up has a price.

But as missionary Nik Ripken asks, "Is Jesus worth it?"

In his book *Through the Eye of a Needle,* historian Peter Brown documents the growth of Christianity from AD 350–550. As the Early Church grew and more Christians participated in local businesses, these business leaders collectively began to play a more significant role in the church's growth throughout the empire.

Historian Paul McKechnie writes in his book *The First Christian Centuries* that during the years of the Early Church, surprisingly, one of the safest places for a Christian to be was in the service of an emperor or public official—right in the eye of the storm! The emperor's servants were actually the ones who ran the empire, so the long-term effects of Christian influence in this context were considerable.

It sounds ironic, considering the persecution that happened all around them, but McKechnie documents that as servants, then assistants, then managers, Christians made remarkable inroads into the palace during the first generation of Christianity. It's a powerful example that sticking it out in antagonistic places can open doors for positive change.

But that only happens if we stay in place.

LIVE YOUR PRINCIPLES,
LOVE YOUR ENEMIES

Few companies have weathered more controversy in the United States lately than Chick-fil-A, the family-owned company started in 1946, when Truett Cathy opened his first restaurant in Hapeville, Georgia. Credited with inventing Chick-fil-A's boneless chicken breast sandwich, today the company boasts more than two thousand locations.

Because of the family's Christian principles, Chick-fil-A has become famous for not opening on Sunday, to allow their employees the day off for church or whatever they choose. However, the company's commitment to the biblical ideal of family has frequently gotten it in hot water. Critics frequently blast the company in the media, and even the mayor of New York City urged people to boycott the restaurant and categorized the company as hateful because of their position on biblical values. They've also been criticized by other municipalities for the same thing.

But rather than respond in the same way, the team at Chick-fil-A is committed to living out their values. On hearing news of the mass shooting in a gay bar in Orlando, the company not only encouraged employees and local citizens to donate blood for the victims but they also did what they do best: they fired up the grill and donated hundreds of sandwiches and fries to victims and their families.

And they did it on a Sunday when their doors were normally closed.

Social media and news organizations picked up the story, and before long, the news was spread across the country of how Chick-fil-A responded to this tragedy. It was a powerful example of loving your enemies while still living your principles.

> When your theology becomes an obstacle to mercy, change your theology.
>
> —PASTOR ANDY STANLEY

There is perhaps no better example of the difference that public and demonstrative love can make than what's happened recently in the Catholic Church. Consider the last two popes—Pope Benedict and Pope Francis. Hardly anyone who isn't a Vatican expert could tell you the differences between them intellectually and theologically. But how they *express* their faith? The two popes couldn't be more different.

What most folks admire about Pope Francis is his *humility*. After generations of popes living in luxury and attended to by an army of assistants, this pope carries his own suitcase, regularly meets with the poor and disadvantaged, and, whenever possible, disregards the showy trappings of his office. He's one of *us*, and that's why so many people respond. Even secular and normally jaded journalists say things like, "I'm not a Catholic, but if I was, I'd want to be like this pope."

Pope Francis's five-day visit to the United States in 2015

captivated the country and the press. It was like the Beatles arriving in America! Keep in mind his visit was in the wake of the massive priest sex abuse scandal that is still in the news, as court settlements continue to mount. But dead center in what could be called a hostile cultural environment, the pope was received by cheering crowds, political leaders lining up to meet him, and fawning media coverage.

That's because Pope Francis is everyone's pope—friend and foe alike.

> On the last day, Jesus will look us over not for medals, diplomas, or honors, but for scars.
>
> —BRENNAN MANNING, *RUTHLESS TRUST*

The handmaid to holiness will always be persecution. It's a fact. But if we remain steadfast in our convictions, endure the hardships, and love our enemies, then the gospel will be victorious.

CHAPTER 18

HOW NOW
SHALL WE LIVE?

Your life as a Christian should make nonbelievers
question their disbelief in God.

PASTOR, AUTHOR, AND THEOLOGIAN
DIETRICH BONHOEFFER

First of all, we need to remember that the Christian
must not act in exactly the same way as everyone else.
He has a part to play in this world which
no one else can possibly fulfill.

JACQUES ELLUL,
THE PRESENCE OF THE KINGDOM

IN HIS BOOK *Bad Religion: How We Became a Nation of Heretics*, *New York Times* columnist Ross Douthat wrote, "In many ways, the landscape of Christianity in America—where the faith is uncorrupted by state power and a thousand heresies are allowed to bloom—resembles the climate of the early Church, with all the furious theological ferment but (mercifully) none of the Roman persecution."

However, in Douthat's view, the twenty-first-century version will have a dramatically different ending. He believes the direction this culture is going needs more moral correction than moral license, more self-examination than self-satisfaction, and more chastisement than comfort.

We agree with the direction Douthat believes our culture is going, and we also believe that—like the days of the Early Church—it's not too late to turn things around and find the way back. But it won't happen if we continue to serve That Other God. That will only hasten our disappearance into the cultural margins.

From the perspective of two people who have spent their careers in media, we believe we can learn from our critics. Through headlines about the erosion of Christian principles from the public square and Christians' loss of credibility in nearly every area of life, our critics force us to continually up our game. A scholar on the history of Christianity, Robert Louis Wilken confirms that the Early Church's critics made a positive difference:

Perhaps this is one large conclusion to be drawn from the study of pagan criticism of Christianity. Christianity became the kind of religion it did because it had critics like Celsus, Porphyry, and Julian. They helped Christians to find their authentic voice, and without them Christianity would have been the poorer.

We wholeheartedly believe that the most searing criticism of Christianity today is that we strayed from our mandate of being salt and light in the world. At the end of the day, it isn't what Christians say but rather how we live that communicates eternal principles to a nonbelieving culture.

WHERE DO WE GO FROM HERE?

We've written this book based on decades of experience understanding how to engage and persuade large groups of people, and our sincere hope is that it will inspire Christians everywhere to live lives that will astonish nonbelievers and eventually lead them to Christ.

As we have seen, boycotts don't work, petition drives don't work, and political campaigns don't work. For too long, Christians have sought out influence and power instead of seeking to love and serve. So how can we take the first steps on the way back to recapturing the attention of our culture in a *good* way, without compromising any of the Bible's doctrinal principles? What the early Christians did that was so mind-blowing is that they loved and served others. They rescued babies, ran to help those affected by the plague, and lived lives that pointed to something better.

They were known for their love and service to people.

What if *we* lived lives that so baffled the culture that we would force people to rethink what they thought about Jesus?

This book isn't a how-to manual or a workbook. We've cited stories from our own experience and the experiences of others, but our goal is to spark your imagination so you can begin your own journey on the way back to a credible faith that will astonish our culture.

Everyone reading this book is different, lives in a unique place, and can find individual opportunities to engage unbelievers every day. We've fallen short time and time again, but we never stop looking for chances to change people's thinking. We've shared a few of our ideas, but ultimately, we'll leave it up to you how you can start engaging and impacting people—in the hope that it will eventually force them to rethink their perceptions and opinions of who we are as a Christian community and who this God is that we serve.

But wherever the journey on the way back leads you, here are a handful of final thoughts that we believe will help.

REIGNITE YOUR SENSE OF WONDER AND ENCHANTMENT

Like most Christians, the world is longing to reconnect with the mystery of the universe. Paraphrasing Blaise Pascal, all of us have a God-shaped hole in our hearts. Yet Christians are often the least creative and imaginative people in the room. We spend more time being annoyed that store employees say, "Happy Holidays" than showing people the wonder that surrounds us. You've heard it said that it's time Christians should stop being *against* everything and start being *for* something. So let's start by reminding those around us of the wonder and mystery we can experience every day.

The world values creativity, and Christians have the capacity to be extraordinarily creative beings. It's no surprise that God chose to introduce Himself to us in the first verse of the Bible as a *Creator*. We are made in His image, so let's begin to express that creativity to the world.

BE A BETTER NEIGHBOR

We regularly receive questions from Christians who want to impact the culture in Hollywood, in Washington, D.C., or other influential centers around the world. But they often forget a place they could start today—their own neighborhood.

One of the most common complaints about our distracted culture is that we've lost real contact with our friends and neighbors. In fact, Pew Research indicates that only 43 percent of Americans even know their neighbors' names. Based on Matthew 22:39, what would it look like if Christians began a serious and strategic campaign to bring our neighborhoods together?

You want to be a missionary? Great. Go next door.

—EVANGELIST J. JOHN

Do you know your own neighbors? Maybe it's time to move beyond the occasional hello to being there for them during difficult times, anticipating needs, and discovering what it means to be a real friend. This will ultimately force your neighbors to wonder about what drives you. Just as the Apartment Life ministry we highlighted in a previous chapter, you could be the catalyst to connect families on your street or in your apartment building. As pastor Dwight L. Moody put it, "Lighthouses blow no horns, they just shine."

When it comes to being a better neighbor, David Apple, author of *Not Just a Soup Kitchen: How Mercy Ministry in the Local Church Transforms Us All*, reminds us that we need to be specific. One book reviewer summarized Apple's book like this:

> Yes, cook a meal for a severely ill mother with three young children, but offer a choice of two courses so she and her family won't have tuna noodle casserole four nights in a row. No, don't say, "Call me any time for anything," because the person in need will probably never call. Yes, make a specific offer, such as "I want to come over Monday at three o'clock to bake cookies and clean your pantry shelf."

We have a friend who gets up early and takes long walks every morning. One day, he started picking up one of his elderly neighbor's newspapers off the grass and leaving it on the porch for him. The neighbor was baffled at how the paper got there each morning, until he woke up early one day and saw who the Good Samaritan was. It was such a small act, yet they've become friends because of the effort.

That experience spurred the two neighbors to launch a block party. They invited everyone on their street, and to their surprise, almost all the neighbors showed up. Now it's become a yearly tradition. It's an example that *sharing your faith is not that hard*. You don't have to start a Bible study or do street witnessing. Just throw a party!

SET THE EXAMPLE WITH YOUR OWN FAMILY

In a world where abortion, same-sex marriage, and gender identity are all hot-button issues, perhaps the greatest way to present the Bible's teaching on marriage and family is simply to be a great example.

Think for a minute how difficult it is in a culture of fractured families for people to really understand the gospel story. How does someone who's never known, or has hated their absent father understand the depth of the eternal Father's love? How would someone in that same situation understand the significance of the nativity or the relationship of the Father, Son, and Holy Spirit? Why should the story of Mary and Joseph matter in a world where marriage is whatever one wants it to be? The Bible is filled with illustrations, parables, and references to family, and without firsthand experience, a reader is simply lost.

> Out of one hundred men, one will read the Bible. The other ninety-nine will read the Christian.
>
> —PASTOR DWIGHT L. MOODY

If the Christian community worked harder at making our marriages and families succeed, it would have enormous impact across the country. In fact, considering the confusion about marriage, gender, and family issues in secular society today, marriage counseling, classes, and support groups could become one of the most fruitful missions of the church.

If the church could become known as the one group in our population who most values marriage, rarely divorces, has amazing families, and offers dignity and worth to all ages and generations, it would become a beacon to a culture looking for answers.

BECOME A PATRON

We often think of a patron of the arts as someone incredibly wealthy. But the dictionary defines *patron* as: "a person who supports with money, gifts, efforts, or endorsement an artist, writer, museum, cause, charity, institution, special event, or the like." Financially supporting someone who has a great gift, vision, or calling is wonderful, but a patron also supports through mentoring, personal effort, endorsements, networking, practical help, or just being a friend.

Think of the talented Christian filmmakers, musicians, artists, writers, and others you know. Perhaps it's a young law student struggling to pay her tuition or a Christian medical student who needs a place to stay. How could your support in one or more of the ways above make a difference for them? No matter what your financial circumstance, career, or position in life, your investment could help a struggling Christian artist, entrepreneur, missionary, or someone else get from where they are to where they need to be.

Being a patron means supporting worthy causes in every direction, not just up. One morning while jogging to his favorite coffee place, Jonathan noticed the extraordinary number of homeless people living in the shadows in the four-mile round trip. So he made the decision to learn the names of every homeless person he could find within walking distance of his house.

Jonathan learned their names and heard their stories. And he discovered it doesn't take much to impact their lives for the better. He started small—a cup of coffee, a sandwich, new socks, a pair of shoes. But that increased to the point where in the last year alone he has helped three people get off the street and begin new lives.

POLITICAL PARTIES BEFORE YOUR FAITH: DON'T DRINK THE WATER

If you ever go to a Third World country, there's a solid piece of advice you should take to heart: don't drink the water. If you've ever made that mistake, then you probably have a thoroughly unpleasant memory of a night spent hugging the porcelain. But in that agonizing process, you learned some things that just shouldn't be experimented with.

The sad reality of twenty-first-century America is that the mixture of party politics and faith is just as explosive (and we don't mean that figuratively). It always ends badly.

Think back—can you recall a single instance in the last twenty years when churches in bed with political parties was a net gain for our faith? When the Christian church becomes allied with a political party, it almost always hurts far more than helps.

The fact is, to govern, politicians *must* compromise. It's the nature of the process, and that's a good thing. But when our faith gets aligned with a political party, those compromises end up making us look like the worst kind of hypocrites. Remember our discussion of "influence" earlier in the book? All those negative connotations are multiplied when Christians are perceived to use their corporate "clout" in the political arena. It's a disaster when it appears the church as a whole has become an extension of the Democratic, Republican, or other party.

The truth of politics is that no party's platform lines up 100 percent of the time with the tenets of Christianity, so neither major party can ever be completely aligned with the Scripture. Christianity tied to party politics needs to go the way of the buggy whip and the fax machine and be a relic of a long-ago past. Instead, while individual Christians can join political parties and be part of the process, the church as a corporate body needs to be a political free agent—focused on *issues* more than parties.

There's no higher or sturdier ledge to stand on than when you understand the difference between the ever-shifting planks of your party for the never-changing rock of your faith. All of a sudden, we'll start finding people like a liberal who is pro-life. A conservative who is opposed to the death penalty. A Red Stater who is for racial justice and radical acts of service and love to the LGBTQ+ community. A Blue Stater who believes marriage between a man and a woman is the highest ideal. What's more, you can't begin to know the freedom you will experience on social media when you unharness yourself and become a free agent for issues! Trust us—your friends and family won't know what to do with you anymore!

To be certain, we believe every Christian can and should be actively involved in politics. God has given us an awesome responsibility to participate in the political system, both as voters and in the governing of people. So by all means, vote, campaign, run for office, and discuss the issues as vigorously as you want. But we should be very concerned when the church itself gets lumped into a political party that only stands for the values of Jesus when it's politically convenient.

And what if you're asked to personally advise the president or other political leaders? Our advice is to absolutely do it. We have a responsibility to pray for our political leaders, and if they honestly request spiritual counsel, then we can do no less than offer it. On the other hand, this is often a trap. Invariably, the Christian leader's sage advice coincidentally is timed to a press release with photo opportunity for the politician. When that happens, the damage to the body of Christ can be significant. When Christian leaders move from spending time in *private* prayer and counsel with a political leader to *public* photo ops, campaign stops, fundraising events, and interviews in the media, something has gotten terribly out of balance.

Don't become a tool.

In his book *Nearing Home,* evangelist Billy Graham lists among things he would change if he had to live his life again: "I also would have steered clear of politics. I'm grateful for the opportunities God gave me to minister to people in high places; people in power have spiritual and personal needs like everyone else, and often they have no one to talk to. But looking back I know I sometimes crossed the line, and I wouldn't do that now."

It's an important lesson from a man of remarkable impact and integrity.

COUNTERACT RACISM
IN THE CHURCH WITH 50/50

There is no question that America has a sorry history of racism. More than fifteen decades since the end of the Civil War and now more than fifty years since the Civil Rights era, the legacy of slavery still casts a long shadow over policing, crime, education, wages, employment opportunities, and a host of other matters. In some of these divisive areas, it often feels like healing might never come at all.

The role of churches in racial reconciliation has been, at best, a mixed bag. In fits and starts, some pastors at a handful of churches have, over the decades, actively pursued bridging the chasm between White and Black America. But fifty years after Martin Luther King Jr. labeled Sunday mornings at eleven "the most segregated hour in America," the statistics reveal a hard truth. While things are slowly improving, 80 percent of churchgoers still attend a church where one race is at least 80 percent of the congregation. At this rate, churches will finally be fully integrated sometime in the twenty-third century.

There is little that individual Christians can do to counteract institutional racism. But there is a lot we can to clean up our own house.

We propose an initiative called 50/50, where two racially

self-segregated churches trade fifty parishioners each for six months. The goal and hope for this initiative is that a percentage of these fifty pioneers never come back home. After six months, the two churches do it again, and they keep sending out these reconciliation missionaries until both churches are substantially more integrated.

Of course, churches need to find willing partners who are relatively similar in size and theological expression and adjust the numbers accordingly. But something radical and extraordinary must be done to shake up the self-segregation that currently exists. Otherwise, the hard-won societal victories for equal rights will have not been manifested in the one place that should have led integration from the start.

DO IT ALL WITH JOY

On a very early morning flight to Nashville recently, Phil sat next to an anxious older lady who obviously wasn't very accustomed to flying. They sat on the first row, and she fumbled with her seatbelt. The person who had flown in the seat on the flight before had used a seatbelt extender. She struggled with it for a moment before Phil leaned over, unbuckled the extension, showed her how to fasten the belt, and as usual, made a joke in the process.

"Well, you're awfully happy this early!" she said. Phil explained that he was a morning person and that the first part of the day was his favorite part. She was baffled at how anyone could be so happy early in the morning, and it started a conversation that naturally led to his reasons for the joy she noticed.

May the God of hope fill you with all joy and peace as you trust in him, so that you may overflow with hope by the power of the Holy Spirit. (Romans 15:13 NIV)

Phil didn't have to figure out how to open up an awkward conversation about God, didn't have to hand her a tract, and didn't have to force the issue. He was simply joyful, and she noticed. That's all it took.

In many ways, possibly the greatest single difference between believers and nonbelievers should be the presence of joy. Even in the most difficult circumstances, Christians should be joyful, and when that happens, people notice. And for the record, joy isn't merely "fun." It isn't necessarily being happy all the time. Author Kay Warren describes joy this way:

Joy is the settled assurance that God is in control of all the details of my life, the quiet confidence that ultimately everything is going to be all right, and the determined choice to praise God in all things.

That attitude alone will visibly separate believers from the nonbelieving culture. From Kay's perspective, joy involves confidence, assurance, determination, and praise. It's not mindless, it's not about laughter (although it could be), and it's not shallow.

A few years ago, the *Los Angeles Times* reported that one in five Americans was taking medication for a mental disorder. Based on reports like that, real joy is something the world knows far too little about, and if we live out what it means on a daily basis, the people around us will notice.

REMEMBER THAT *GOD'S* PRIORITIES AREN'T ALWAYS *OUR* PRIORITIES

During the editing of our feature film on the worship band Hillsong UNITED, called *Hillsong—Let Hope Rise,* Jonathan set up a meeting with a major studio to discuss a potential theatrical release. To distribute the movie in theaters across America and the world was critical not only to the success of the film but also for sharing its message with as many people as possible. So for the meeting, Jonathan prepared a massive handout, as well as a PowerPoint presentation. He put enormous effort into being ready for that appointment.

The morning of the big meeting, Jon woke up early as usual and was reading his Bible and praying. Not surprisingly, he asked God for favor with the film. But as he was earnestly praying for God to bless the meeting and for it to be successful, in his spirit, he clearly sensed God saying, *Don't worry; the meeting will be fine. Now, let me tell you what I really want you to do. I want you to start a Bible study with the neighbors on your street.*

Jon's first thought was, *Wait a second, God. You don't understand; we're talking about the movie!* But God didn't let up. The change of subject was surprising, even shocking, considering how important the upcoming film distribution meeting would be. But God reminded him that starting a neighborhood Bible study was far more important to *Him.*

God's economy is not our economy. His priorities aren't ours. We must be open—and obedient—to that startling reality.

DON'T GIVE UP!

In all truth, there's nothing we would have loved better than to discover the only problem facing the church was that it needed a new advertising slogan, marketing campaign, or social media push. After all, that's what we do for a living. It would have made writing this book easy!

We've discovered together the problem is much deeper, and it goes right to the root of our hearts.

As we come to the end of our journey together, we hope this book has, to a certain degree, wounded you. Keep in mind that doctors wound us, too, when they cut out a malignant growth. Personal trainers wound us by breaking down our muscles.

Love never comes without wounds; faith never comes without failure.

—ERWIN RAPHAEL MCMANUS, THE ARTISAN SOUL

But just as much as wounding you, we hope this book has started the healing process. It's our deepest longing to see us all start taking the way back, and we sincerely hope this book has inspired you to chase down the faith of our fathers. We promise it's real, but only if you're willing to search relentlessly for it.

Know that millions of men and women before you, in their own time and place in history, walked the exhilarating and lonely path you walk now. Take strength and solace in knowing you are on the same road as the legends of our faith. They, too, climbed and stumbled. They felt fear and triumph—often in the same day. They also gave up sometimes, but they eventually started over. They all passed this way on the journey, just like you.

> The Christian life is not a constant high. I have my moments of deep discouragement. I have to go to God in prayer with tears in my eyes, and say, "O God, forgive me, or help me."
>
> —EVANGELIST BILLY GRAHAM

In those times where you feel the urge to give in, sometimes all you can count on are the friends around you. Find a band of fellow travelers to support you along the way.

If you need some inspiration, look to people who are doing it right. For example, every year, *WORLD* magazine gives Hope Awards to people and organizations who are doing what we have talked about in this book. They are running to the hurting and living out their faith by serving others. These Christian groups don't use government support but do their life-transforming service to others out of compassion. Kudos to *WORLD* magazine for highlighting and celebrating Christians who are doing it right!

Lastly, know that you aren't ever alone. The men and women of the past who have completed the journey before you are rooting you on every step of the way. All of heaven roars at even your smallest victories, and they still willingly cheer your name in your most humiliating defeats. They are true fans.

Make no mistake: to walk away from That Other God and to take the first steps on the way back to a credible, culture-transforming faith will be the hardest steps of your life. After all, you're walking away from the idol your ego demanded you create. But it is our fervent prayer that you quickly discover you've got a Friend on the journey with you, and that He will be there every step of the way.

And be sure of this: I am with you always, even to the end of the age.

—MATTHEW 28:20 NLT

REVIEW

The challenge will be developing ways that honor Christ,
while loving and living with those who think differently.
And that's our new and great challenge. . . .
If we are not a moral majority, how do we show and share
Jesus in the cultural moment where we find ourselves?
Somehow, as God's people, that's how we should
engage culture—that because of our good works they
might glorify God (1 Peter 2:12) and, ultimately,
might consider the truth claims and gospel
and the Christian worldview that undergirds it.

MISSIOLOGIST AND RESEARCHER ED STETZER

SURRENDER

- Is Jesus really the number one priority in my life?
- What are examples?
- How often this week have I allowed outside distractions to become my first priority?

SCRIPTURE

- How many times this week have I spent significant time in the Word of God? Is that amount of time growing as time goes by?
- How often do I explore Scripture for answers before I consult other sources?
- Am I reading randomly, or do I have a structured guide to help me study?

SUBMISSION

- Am I honestly submitted to the authority of Scripture?
- Do I respect and submit to my pastor's authority?
- Am I submitted to my spouse and family?

SERVICE

- How do my actions reflect my faith?
- What have I done this week for someone who could never pay me back?
- Do I have any friends who can do absolutely nothing for me?
- Do my nonbelieving friends notice that there is something different about my life?

SACRIFICE

- Is there anything in my life that has a stronger hold on me than Jesus?
- Would I be willing to answer God's call even if I knew it meant losing everything?
- When was the last time I fasted or gave up something important in exchange for finding a deeper relationship with God?

SIMPLICITY

- Do material things have the right priority in my life?
- Does work, food, alcohol, hobbies, possessions, or anything else stand between me and God?
- What can I give up that might be a distraction from loving others?
- What does my bank account say about my Christian life?

SUFFERING

- How often am I sharing my faith with others?
- Have I done anything this week to help those being persecuted in other places?

FOR FURTHER READING

Addison, Steve. *Movements That Change the World: Five Keys to Spreading the Gospel.* Downers Grove, IL: IVP, 2011.

Barna Trends 2017: What's New and What's Next at the Intersection of Faith and Culture? Grand Rapids: Baker, 2016.

Barna, George and David Kinnaman, eds. *Churchless: Understanding Today's Unchurched and How to Connect with Them.* Carol Stream, IL: Tyndale, 2014.

Battaglia, Joe. *The Politically Incorrect Jesus: Living Boldly in a Culture of Unbelief.* Racine, WI: BroadStreet, 2014.

Bonhoeffer, Dietrich. *Ethics.* Edited by Eberhard Bethge. New York: Simon & Schuster, 2002.

Brown, Peter. *Through the Eye of a Needle: Wealth, the Fall of Rome, and the Making of Christianity in the West, 350–550 AD.* Princeton, NJ: Princeton University Press, 2012.

Burleigh, Michael. *Sacred Causes: The Clash of Religion and Politics, from the Great War to the War on Terror.* New York: HarperCollins, 2007.

Buster, Bobette. *Do Story: How to Tell Your Story So the World Listens.* London: Do Books, 2013.

Caine, Christine. *Undaunted: Daring to Do What God Calls You to Do.* Grand Rapids: Zondervan, 2012.

Campolo, Tony. *Let Me Tell You a Story.* Nashville: Thomas Nelson, 2000.

Challies, Tim. *The Next Story: Life and Faith After the Digital Explosion*. Grand Rapids: Zondervan, 2011.

Chambers, Oswald. *My Utmost for His Highest*. Grand Rapids: Discovery House, 2014.

Chesterton, G. K. *In Defense of Sanity: The Best Essays of G.K. Chesterton*. San Francisco: Ignatius Press, 2011.

Cialdini, Robert B. *Influence: The Psychology of Persuasion*. New York: William Morrow, 1993.

Claiborne, Shane. *The Irresistible Revolution: Living as an Ordinary Radical*. Grand Rapids: Zondervan, 2016.

Cooke, Phil. *Unique: Telling Your Story in the Age of Brands and Social Media*. Grand Rapids: Baker, 2015.

Courtney, Jeremy. *Preemptive Love*. Nashville: Howard, 2014.

Crouch, Andy. *Culture Making: Recovering Our Creative Calling*. Downers Grove, IL: IVP, 2008.

D'Souza, Dinesh. *What's So Great About Christianity*. Carol Stream, IL: Tyndale, 2007.

Detweiler, Craig. *iGods: How Technology Shapes our Spiritual and Social Lives*. Ada, MI: Brazos, 2013.

Douthat, Ross. *Bad Religion: How We Became a Nation of Heretics*. New York: Free Press, 2012.

Downs, Tim. *Finding Common Ground: How to Communicate with Those Outside the Christian Community, While We Still Can*. Chicago: Moody, 1999.

Drane, John William. *Cultural Change and Biblical Faith: The Future of the Church; Biblical and Missiological Essays for the New Century*. Waynesboro, GA: Paternoster, 2000.

Dreher, Rod. *The Benedict Option: A Strategy for Christians in a Post-Christian Nation*. New York: Sentinel, 2017.

Dunn-Wilson, David. *A Mirror for the Church: Preaching in the First Five Centuries*. Grand Rapids: Eerdmans, 2005.

Eberstadt, Mary. *How the West Really Lost God: A New Theory of Secularization.* West Conshohocken, PA: Templeton Press, 2013.

Eberstadt, Mary. *It's Dangerous to Believe: Religious Freedom and Its Enemies.* New York: Harper, 2016.

Ellul, Jacques. *Propaganda: The Formation of Men's Attitudes.* New York: Vintage Books, 2005.

Ellul, Jacques. *The Presence of the Kingdom.* Colorado Springs: Helmers & Howard, 1989.

Ellul, Jacques. *The Subversion of Christianity.* Grand Rapids: Eerdmans, 1991.

Forster, Greg. *Joy for the World: How Christianity Lost Its Cultural Influence and Can Begin Rebuilding It.* Wheaton, IL: Crossway, 2014.

Foster, Richard. *Celebration of Discipline.* San Francisco: HarperSanFrancisco, 1988.

Frankl, Viktor E. *Man's Search for Meaning.* Boston: Beacon, 2014.

Franklin, DeVon. *Produced by Faith: Enjoy Real Success without Losing Your True Self.* Nashville: Howard, 2012.

Gladwell, Malcolm. *David and Goliath: Underdogs, Misfits, and the Art of Battling Giants.* New York: Back Bay Books, 2015.

Goff, Bob. *Love Does: Discover a Secretly Incredible Life in an Ordinary World.* Nashville: Thomas Nelson, 2012.

Gottschall, Jonathan. *The Storytelling Animal: How Stories Make Us Human.* New York: Mariner Books, 2012.

Graham, Jack. *Unseen: Angels, Satan, Heaven, Hell, and Winning the Battle for Eternity.* Minneapolis: Bethany House, 2013.

Green, Steve, and Todd Hillard. *The Bible in America: What We Believe About the Most Important Book in Our History.* Oklahoma City: Dust Jacket Press, 2013.

Greenfield, Craig. *Subversive Jesus: An Adventure in Justice, Mercy, and Faithfulness in a Broken World* Grand Rapids: Zondervan, 2016.

Guinness, Os. *A Free People's Suicide: Sustainable Freedom and the American Future.* Downers Grove, IL: IVP, 2012.

Guinness, Os. *Renaissance: The Power of the Gospel However Dark the Times.* Downers Grove, IL: InterVarsity, 2014.

Guinness, Os. *The Last Christian on Earth: Uncover the Enemy's Plot to Undermine the Church.* Ventura, CA: Regal, 2010.

Gutsche, Jeremy. *Exploiting Chaos: 150 Ways to Spark Innovation During Times of Change.* New York: Gotham Books, 2009.

Hansen, Ron. *A Stay Against Confusion: Essays on Faith and Fiction.* New York: HarperCollins, 2001.

Hellerman, Joseph H. *Embracing Shared Ministry: Power and Status in the Early Church and Why It Matters Today.* Grand Rapids: Kregel, 2013.

Hewitt, Hugh. *In, But Not Of: A Guide to Christian Ambition and the Desire to Influence the World.* Nashville: Thomas Nelson, 2003.

Hipps, Shane. *Flickering Pixels: How Technology Shapes Your Faith.* Grand Rapids: Zondervan, 2009.

His Holiness John Paul II. *Crossing the Threshold of Hope.* New York: Knopf, 1995.

Hoskins, Rob. *Hope Delivered: Affecting Destiny Through the Power of God's Word.* Lake Mary, FL: Passio, 2012.

Houston, Brian. *Live Love Lead: Your Best Is Yet to Come!* New York: Faith Words, 2015.

Hunter, James Davison. *To Change the World: The Irony, Tragedy, and Possibility of Christianity in the Late Modern World.* New York: Oxford University Press, 2010.

Hurtado, Larry W. *Destroyer of the gods: Early Christian Distinctiveness in the Roman World.* Waco, TX: Baylor University Press, 2017.

Inchausti, Robert. *Subversive Orthodoxy: Outlaws, Revolutionaries, and Other Christians in Disguise.* Grand Rapids: Brazos Press, 2005.

Inglis, Fred. *A Short History of Celebrity.* Princeton, NJ: Princeton University Press, 2010.

Johnston, Jeremiah. *Unanswered: Lasting Truth for Trending Questions.* New Kensington, PA: Whitaker House, 2011.

Johnston, Robert K. *God's Wider Presence: Reconsidering General Revelation.* Grand Rapids: Baker Academic, 2014.

Keller, Timothy. *The Prodigal God: Recovering the Heart of the Christian Faith.* New York: Viking, 2008.

Keller, Timothy. *The Reason for God: Belief in an Age of Skepticism.* New York: Dutton, 2008.

Kennedy, D. James, and Jerry Newcombe. *What if the Bible Had Never Been Written?* Nashville: Thomas Nelson, 1998.

Kinnaman, David, and Gabe Lyons. *Good Faith: Being a Christian When Society Thinks You're Irrelevant and Extreme.* Grand Rapids: Baker, 2016.

Kubicek, Jeremie. *Leadership Is Dead: How Influence Is Reviving It.* New York: Howard, 2011.

Labberton, Mark. *Called: The Crisis and Promise of Following Jesus Today.* Downers Grove, IL: IVP, 2014.

Llosa, Mario Vargas. *Notes on the Death of Culture: Essays on Spectacle and Society.* Translated by John King. New York: Farrar, Straus and Giroux, 2015.

Lomenick, Brad. *H3 Leadership: Be Humble. Stay Hungry. Always Hustle.* Nashville: Thomas Nelson, 2016.

Lyons, Gabe. *The Next Christians: The Good News About the End of Christian America*. New York: Doubleday Religion, 2010.

Manning, Brennan. *The Importance of Being Foolish: How to Think Like Jesus*. San Francisco: HarperSanFrancisco, 2005.

Marshall, Paul A., Roberta Green Ahmanson, and Lela Gilbert, eds. *Blind Spot: When Journalists Don't Get Religion*. New York: Oxford University Press, 2009.

McGrath, Alister E. *The Twilight of Atheism: The Rise and Fall of Disbelief in the Modern World*. New York: Doubleday, 2008.

McKechnie, Paul R. *The First Christian Centuries: Perspectives on the Early Church*. Downers Grove, IL: InterVarsity, 2001.

McManus, Erwin Raphael. *Uprising: A Revolution of the Soul*. Nashville: Thomas Nelson, 2003.

Metaxas, Eric. *Bonhoeffer: Pastor, Martyr, Prophet, Spy*. Nashville: Thomas Nelson, 2011.

Moore, Russell. *Onward: Engaging the Culture Without Losing the Gospel*. Nashville: B&H, 2015.

Moorhouse, Geoffrey. *The Missionaries*. Philadelphia: J.B. Lippincott, 1973.

Noll, Mark A. *Turning Points: Decisive Moments in the History of Christianity*. Grand Rapids: Baker, 2000.

Nouwen, Henri. *The Selfless Way of Christ: Downward Mobility and the Spiritual Life*. UK: Orbis, 2011.

Nyquist, J. Paul, and Carson Nyquist. *The Post-Church Christian: Dealing with the Generational Baggage of Our Faith*. Chicago: Moody, 2013.

Ortberg, John. *Who Is This Man?: The Unpredictable Impact of the Inescapable Jesus*. Grand Rapids: Zondervan, 2012.

Pearce, Joseph. *Literary Converts: Spiritual Inspiration in an Age of Unbelief*. San Francisco: Ignatius Press, 2006.

Petersen, William J., and Randy Petersen. *100 Christian Books That Changed the Century.* Grand Rapids: F. H. Revell, 2000.

Pettegree, Andrew. *Brand Luther: 1517, Printing, and the Making of the Reformation.* New York: Penguin, 2015.

Phillips, J. B. *Your God Is Too Small.* New York: Touchstone, 2004.

Platt, David. *Counter Culture: A Compassionate Call To Counter Culture in a World of Poverty, Same-Sex Marriage, Racism, Sex Slavery, Immigration, Abortion, Persecution, Orphans, and Pornography.* Carol Stream, IL: Tyndale, 2015.

Platt, David. *Radical: Taking Back Your Faith from the American Dream.* Colorado Springs: Multnomah, 2010.

Poland, Larry W. *Chasm: Crossing the Divide Between Hollywood and People of Faith.* New York: Morgan James, 2014.

Pressfield, Steven. *The Warrior Ethos.* Np: Black Irish Books, 2011.

Reid, T. R. *The United States of Europe: The New Superpower and the End of American Supremacy.* New York: Penguin, 2004.

Reno, Russell R. *In the Ruins of the Church: Sustaining Faith in an Age of Diminished Christianity.* Grand Rapids: Brazos Press, 2002.

Reynolds, David S. *Mightier Than the Sword: Uncle Tom's Cabin and the Battle for America.* New York: Norton, 2011.

Ripken, Nik, and Gregg Lewis. *The Insanity of God: A True Story of Faith Resurrected.* Nashville: B&H, 2013.

Ruden, Sarah. *Paul Among the People: The Apostle Reinterpreted and Reimagined in His Own Time.* New York: Random House, 2010.

Samples, Kenneth R. *7 Truths That Changed the World: Discovering Christianity's Most Dangerous Ideas.* Grand Rapids: Baker, 2012.

Sayers, Dorothy L. *Letters to a Diminished Church: Passionate Arguments for the Relevance of Christian Doctrine.* Nashville: W Publishing Group, 2004.

Scruton, Roger. *Modern Culture.* London: Continuum, 2005.

Scruton, Roger. *The Soul of the World.* Princeton, NJ: Princeton University Press, 2014.

Smith, James K. A. *How (Not) to Be Secular: Reading Charles Taylor.* Grand Rapids: Eerdmans, 2014.

Smith, Judah. *Jesus Is _____.* Nashville: Thomas Nelson, 2013.

Smith, Warren Cole, and John Stonestreet. *Restoring All Things: God's Audacious Plan to Save the World Through Everyday People.* Grand Rapids: Baker, 2015.

Stark, Rodney. *How the West Won: The Neglected Story of the Triumph of Modernity.* Wilmington, DE: ISI Books, 2015.

Stark, Rodney. *The Rise of Christianity: How the Obscure, Marginal Jesus Movement Became the Dominant Religious Force in the Western World in a Few Centuries.* New York: HarperOne, 1997.

Stark, Rodney. *The Triumph of Christianity: How the Jesus Movement Became the World's Largest Religion.* New York: HarperOne, 2011.

Stark, Rodney. *The Victory of Reason: How Christianity Led to Freedom, Capitalism, and Western Success.* New York: Random House, 2005.

Taylor, Charles. *A Secular Age.* Cambridge, MA: Belknap Press of Harvard University Press, 2007.

Tozer, A. W. *The Pursuit of God.* Abbotsford, WI: Aneko Press, 2015.

Tozer, A. W. *Culture: Living as Citizens of Heaven on Earth; Collected Insights from A. W. Tozer.* Chicago: Moody, 2016.

Voskamp, Ann. *One Thousand Gifts: A Dare to Live Fully Right Where You Are.* Grand Rapids: Zondervan, 2011.

Weigel, George. *The Cube and the Cathedral: Europe, America, and Politics Without God.* New York: Basic Books, 2006.

Whitehead, John W. *Religious Apartheid: The Separation of Religion from American Public Life.* Chicago: Moody, 1994.

Wiesel, Elie. *Night.* New York: Hill and Wang, 2006.

Wilberforce, William and Bob Beltz. *Real Christianity: A Paraphrase in Modern English of a Practical View of the Prevailing Religious System of Professed Christians in the Higher and Middle Classes in This Country, Contrasted with Real Christianity.* Published in 1797 by William Wilberforce, Esq. member of Parliament for the county of York. Edited by Bob Beltz. Ventura, CA: Regal, 2006.

Wilken, Robert Louis. *The Christians as the Romans Saw Them.* New Haven, CT: Yale University Press, 2003.

Willard, Dallas. *The Divine Conspiracy: Rediscovering Our Hidden Life in God.* New York: Harper, 1998.

Youssef, Michael. *When the Crosses Are Gone: Restoring Sanity to a World Gone Mad.* NP: Kobri, 2011.

Yun, Brother, and Paul Hattaway. *The Heavenly Man: The Remarkable True Story of Chinese Christian Brother Yun.* Grand Rapids: Kregel, 2002.

Zahnd, Brian. *Sinners in the Hands of a Loving God.* Colorado Springs: Waterbrook, 2017.

ABOUT PHIL COOKE

According to former CNN journalist Paula Zahn, filmmaker and media consultant Phil Cooke is rare—a working producer in Hollywood with a PhD in theology. He's the author of *One Big Thing: Discovering What You Were Born to Do* and *Unique: Telling Your Story in the Age of Brands and Social Media*. He's appeared on NBC, MSNBC, CNBC, CNN, Fox News, and his work has been profiled in the *New York Times*, the *Los Angeles Times*, and the *Wall Street Journal*. He's lectured at universities like Yale, University of California at Berkeley, and UCLA. In addition to writing his blog philcooke.com, he also blogs for the *Huffington Post*, and has been a contributor to *Fast Company*, Forbes.com, Wired.com, and FoxNews.com. Phil is a member of the Academy of Television Arts & Sciences and the Producers Guild of America.

ABOUT JONATHAN BOCK

Jonathan Bock began his career in marketing at Warner Bros. He's the founder and president of Grace Hill Media, which has marketed more than five hundred major motion pictures and television projects to Christian audiences worldwide. He is the producer of *Hillsong—Let Hope Rise,* which chronicles the meteoric rise of the Australian worship band, Hillsong UNITED. He is a member of the Producers Guild of America (PGA) and an elder at Bel Air Church in Los Angeles.

...NJOYED THIS BOOK, WILL YOU CONSIDER ...ARING THE MESSAGE WITH OTHERS?

Mention the book in a blog post or through Facebook, Twitter, or upload a picture through Instagram.

Recommend this book to those in your small group, book club, workplace, and classes.

Head over to facebook.com/worthypublishing, "LIKE" the page, and post a comment as to what you enjoyed the most.

Tweet "I recommend reading #TheWayBack by @PhilCooke @JonathanBock // @worthypub"

Pick up a copy for someone you know who would be challenged and encouraged by this message.

Write a book review online.

Visit us at worthypublishing.com

twitter.com/worthypub

instagram.com/worthypub

facebook.com/worthypublishing

youtube.com/worthypublishing